"The profoundly moving story of a family which has experienced both terrible tragedy and amazing blessing, and has seen the providential hand of God guiding them through. It will give hope and encouragement to many."
Nicky Gumbel, pioneer of the Alpha course and Vicar of Holy Trinity, Brompton, London

"Wes Richards has beautifully and brilliantly written one of the most moving stories you are likely to come across. This book will bring great comfort to those in bereavement and to those who want to know how to sympathize with those in grief. I urge its wide circulation."
R. T. Kendall, author and former minister, Westminster Chapel, London

"I've known Wes for nearly a quarter of a century, as my pastor, as my 'elder brother', as a close friend. Every time I turned to him, he would find ways to counsel and inspire me in the midst of the pain and suffering that he and his family experienced. It's easy to become blasé, even cynical. Wes reminds us why we shouldn't."
J.P. Rangaswami, Chief Scientist for salesforce.com and blogger at confusedofcalcutta.com

"With a vibrant narrative, so characteristic of his personality, Pastor Wes takes us through each episode of his life. Hope and a Future *is an inspiring book that will motivate your faith."*
César Castellanos, Senior Pastor of the 150,000-member Misión Carismática Internacional (MCI) church, Bogotá, Colombia, and pioneer of the G12 vision

"An amazing example of overcoming in the most difficult situations. The way that Pastor Wes describes ⌷⌷⌷⌷⌷ *heart. I really enjoyed it. It's a boo*⌷ *reads it."*
Manuela Castellanos, Pastor, ⌷

"I have known Wes and the family for many years. Hope and a Future *is an account of God's abundant grace through times of death and incredible hardship. It's a powerful testimony; real, credible and good. Everyone who wants to grow in maturity should buy this book."*
Ken Costa, Chairman of Alpha International, investment banker and former chairman of Lazard International

"It always gives me great pleasure to endorse any book that is written about family with the sole purpose of bringing glory to Jesus Christ. I pray that Hope and a Future *will encourage many families that are going through times of testing."*
Angus Buchan, speaker and author of *Faith Like Potatoes*

ABOUT THE AUTHOR

WES RICHARDS HAS BEEN a pastor for over thirty-five years. He was previously a journalist with an evening newspaper as a leader and feature writer. He is the Senior Pastor of King's Church International, a non-denominational church based in Windsor, England. He has a Master's degree in Theology from the London School of Theology and wrote his dissertation on "The Global Holy Spirit Movement".

He travels widely and is a regular speaker at international conferences.

He was married for twenty-eight years to Carol, who died in 2002. He has two sons and a daughter and eight grandchildren.

You can follow Wes Richards at:
> Twitter: @wescast
> Facebook: facebook.com/wesrichards
> or contact him at wrichards@hopeandafuture.info

To see more about this book, go to:
> www.hopeandafuture.info
> Facebook: facebook.com/HopeAndAFuture

HOPE AND A FUTURE

A STORY OF LOVE, LOSS, AND LIVING AGAIN

WES RICHARDS

MONARCH
BOOKS

Oxford, UK & Grand Rapids, Michigan, USA

Published by Monarch Books
an imprint of
Lion Hudson plc
Wilkinson House, Jordan Hill Road, Oxford OX2 8DR, England
Tel: +44 (0)1865 302750 Fax: +44 (0)1865 302757
Email: monarch@lionhudson.com
www.lionhudson.com/monarch

ISBN 978 0 85721 291 7
e-ISBN 978 0 85721 402 7

First edition 2012

Acknowledgments
Scripture quotations taken from the Holy Bible, New International Version Anglicised. Copyright © 1979, 1984, 2011 Biblica, formerly International Bible Society. Used by permission of Hodder & Stoughton Ltd, an Hachette UK company. All rights reserved. "NIV" is a registered trademark of Biblica. UK trademark number 1448790. Scripture quotations marked NKJV taken from the New King James Version. Copyright © 1982 by Thomas Nelson, Inc. Used by permission. All rights reserved.
Song on page 88:
When You Believe
from THE PRINCE OF EGYPT
Words and Music by Stephen Schwartz
Copyright © 1997 DWA Songs (ASCAP)
Worldwide Rights for DWA Songs Administered by BMG Rights Management (US) LLC
International Copyright Secured All Rights Reserved
Reprinted by Permission of Hal Leonard Corporation
Quotations on p 111 taken from A Grief Observed by C. S. Lewis copyright © C. S. Lewis Pte. Ltd. 1951. Extracts reprinted by permission.
Quotation on p 126 taken from Mere Christianity by C. S. Lewis copyright © C. S. Lewis Pte. Ltd. 1942, 1943, 1944, 1952. Extract reprinted by permission.
Song on pp 218–219: You Are My Strength. Words & Music by Reuben Morgan © 2007 Hillsong Music Publishing. All rights reserved. International copyright secured. Used by permission.

A catalogue record for this book is available from the British Library.

Printed and bound in the UK, August 2012, LH26.

To Carol
For her love, life and legacy
...and the grandchildren who came after her:
Samuel, Joseph, Joshua, Joel, Isaac, Daniel,
Caleb, Eliana and...

CONTENTS

ACKNOWLEDGMENTS

E NCOURAGEMENT is one of life's greatest gifts. This book is, in many ways, the product of many people who have encouraged me.

I would like to thank Jonathan Aitken for his friendship and for helping me to believe that I should, could and would write this book. He not only inspired me by his words and his own well documented story of comeback after his very public political downfall. He also encouraged me by his willingness to take time to diligently and patiently mentor me as an author. I am grateful that he held me accountable to write 400 words a day, five days a week.

I would like to thank publisher Tony Collins for showing faith in me as a first time author and for his warmth and integrity. Thanks also to Jenny Ward who oversaw the whole editorial process and for everyone from the publishing team to distributors and bookshop staff who each played their part to put this book into your hands.

Thanks to Guy McDonnell and Keith Danby for their part in linking me up with Monarch/Lion Hudson plc.

Thanks to Paola Rodriguez for her encouragement and sharp administrative support, to Nadia Bramley for getting permissions for quotations and lyrics and to Paula Lavender for the early proofreading.

Thanks to my son James for all his creative ideas, particularly with the cover design, and for the input from James Williams,

Raul Arevalo, and Monarch's Roger Chouler. Thanks to Wesley for helping synchronize the initial editorial process. Thanks to Mel for her daughterly and wise insights on this book.

Thanks to all who have kindly written commendations.

Thanks to Colombian pastor César Castellanos whose outstanding pastoral compassion was a turning point in my life, and to all the Castellanos family for their example, friendship, and leadership.

Thanks to my American family, the Peters of St Louis. We have been friends for thirty years and Pete and Linda have stood with us through everything.

Thanks to William and Stella, and all the Joutet family in France, for their ongoing kindness and a friendship that now spans four generations.

Thanks to everyone, both at home and abroad, including many wonderful doctors and medical staff, who helped us in so many different ways during the nightmare of Carol's illness.

Thanks to Ken and Lois Gott, their family and church for all their love and care at our most vulnerable time.

I am thankful also for all the blessings of having "family", friends and fellow leaders in South Africa, Sri Lanka, Singapore, Sweden, Colombia, Peru, Burkina Faso, France, The Netherlands, Romania, Portugal, Australia, the Middle East, Canada, the USA and the UK. I hope this book encourages you as you have encouraged me.

I am so grateful also for the love and commitment of many great people in the King's Church International family in Robertson.

A big thanks to my King's Church International family based in Windsor. Some, like my stalwart friends Terry and Margaret Beasley, George and Carole Shaw, J.P. and Shane Rangaswami, and others, are mentioned in this book. But I would need another book to mention everyone. So to every faithful leader, church member and staff member, thank you for all your love, prayers and support. You are truly great people. Take a hug and take a bow. It's an honour to be your Senior Pastor.

And of course I am so thankful for all my family. This book is their story, not just my story. I thank God for two lovely, caring daughters-in-law, Wilana and Vasti, a very kind and gifted son-in-law, Drikus, and their loving parents, my "adopted" and always hospitable brother and sister, Gert and Lina who first welcomed us to South Africa.

As for my grandchildren, they are all characters. As they grow I want each one of them to fully appreciate the blessings of their unique family history, to be secure in their individual identity, and to maximize the fruitful destiny that God has for each of them. I love them and bless them.

Through everything my three children, Wesley, James and Melody have been rock-like in their love and concern for me and each other. I owe each of them so much. I am as proud to be their father as Carol was delighted to be their mother.

They were Carol's life work and they are her greatest achievement. I am grateful they had such a Mum and that I had such a wife.

For each and every blessing, past, present and future, I thank God for His goodness and amazing grace.

FOREWORD

THIS BOOK FIRST ENTERED my consciousness during a winter afternoon walk around Windsor Great Park a day or two after Christmas 2007. I had just enjoyed a relaxed lunch with Wes and his extended family of children and grandchildren. Yet for all the *joie de vivre* in the home, I knew that Wes was still grieving for his beloved wife Carol, the maternal rock of their family, who had so sadly and prematurely died of cancer a few years earlier.

As we strode across the landscape of the park, with Windsor Castle behind us in the distance, it was natural to talk about Carol. Wes described the human dramas she embodied – those of love, laughter, courage, medical disappointment, suffering, acceptance, death and spiritual renewal within the family. There were as many mood changes in our conversation as there were scene changes on the walk. Inspiration must have been somewhere in the air, for eventually I said, "You know, there's a book in this."

"But I've never been an author," replied Wes. "Will you help me write it?"

As it turned out, I did not write a single word of *Hope and a Future*. But I did spend a fair bit of time with my friend the novice author, commenting on, occasionally criticizing but most often praising his early drafts. As the manuscript took shape I became gripped by it. For this is a compelling narrative of raw human emotion. Although Carol's terminal illness is at its heart, the humour and the happy family life are the limbs, perhaps even the wings, of the unfolding story. Transcending it all are the everlasting hands of God, guiding every step of the journey.

I will not spoil the suspense by providing trailer-like glimpses of this powerfully moving and deeply spiritual saga. What I will highlight is the inspiration and encouragement this intensely personal account can give to anyone who has to pass through life's darker valleys of loss, pain and brokenness. Knowing these depths all too well myself, I recognize that Wes Richards has set down in these pages some memorable footprints. In the words of Henry Longfellow, may they be:

> *Footprints, that perhaps another,*
> *Sailing o'er life's solemn main,*
> *A forlorn and shipwrecked brother,*
> *Seeing, shall take heart again.*[1]

Jonathan Aitken
Author and former British Cabinet minister

---

1   Henry Longfellow (1807–1882).

INTRODUCTION

E VERYBODY WANTS TO HOPE. But maybe you are one of the many people who are struggling to hope. Life has been just too bad or too sad for you to dare to dream that you could ever again have a hope-filled future.

Hope, as President Obama expressed it, is an audacious concept. But how can you hope when you have had more than your share of bitter experiences? How can you hope when you have lost your loved ones? How can you hope when there is so much mess and carnage in the world?

Hope, however, is a treasure worth guarding. Hope is powerful enough to triumph over great setbacks.

History is full of examples of people and even nations who have continued to hope even when everything seemed hopeless. Sir Winston Churchill had it right when he defied the prospect of looming disaster to declare that Britain's darkest time would prove to be its finest hour.

It takes faith and courage to hope for any kind of a future when life has hit you hard. I have witnessed many challenges to hope in over four decades as a journalist and as a pastor.

Some time ago I conducted the funeral of a well-loved, apparently fit, twenty-eight-year-old young man from our church who died suddenly and unaccountably in his sleep, leaving a wife who was five months pregnant with their first child.

Around that period I was introduced to a long-time and happily married couple and their four kids in their teens and twenties. A few days later I was told that this close-knit family and many others in their home town had been shattered by the news that the father had been shot and killed when thieves broke into their holiday home.

When darkness falls with such brutality and finality, hope seems forever lost. More times than I care to remember, I have sat and wept alongside people as they have battled to believe that the sun will ever shine again.

I know how that feels, not only pastorally but also personally. On one beautiful English summer's afternoon, 29 June 2002, a very big light went out in my life when my darling wife and best friend for thirty-four years lost her fight with cancer.

I was simply heartbroken. And so too were our three children and many family members and friends.

My Christian faith reassured me that I was not without hope, even in the midst of great pain. But I had little idea how this could apply to us practically.

Each of us knew that life would never be the same again. For all the well-meaning words of friends, it was crushingly obvious that our lives could not somehow be neatly put back together as if nothing had happened.

From here on we were in uncharted territory and we were not at all sure that we had enough strength for the journey into the unknown.

Yet what lay ahead was to confirm the gutsy old adage that "It's always too soon to quit." More than that, what we were to discover brought into vivid focus the biblical promise that we had a "hope and a future".

These words were originally declared by the Hebrew prophet Jeremiah to a people who had been weighed down by years of misery. They needed some major convincing that there could be any good times ahead for them.

Little by little we realized that this prospect of a positive future after a negative past was also relevant to us, as it is to all who know what it is to be caught up in dislocated circumstances beyond our control.

If that includes you, then I hope this book will encourage and help you. I could never have foreseen how our story would unfold after so much sadness. When we were at our lowest moments we found that our story was not over. Far from it.

Your story is not over either.

PROLOGUE

Cape Town International Airport, 15 November 2002

L OVE WAS UNMISTAKABLY in the air as we approached the arrivals hall early one sunny spring morning. Our host, Gert Erasmus, was waiting to welcome us on our first trip to South Africa. So too was his extremely pretty, tanned and casually dressed twenty-one-year-old daughter, Vasti.

I greeted them warmly enough, as did my daughter Melody. But out of the corner of my eye I noticed that my second son James, aged twenty-two, was hugging Vasti for a number of seconds longer than protocol strictly demanded. Up till then they had only had a brief acquaintance. From that moment they were inseparable.

After three days spent with families and friends, James came to me for a chat. "Dad, I've found my wife!" he said, stating what was obvious to anybody who saw them.

Just over a year later they were married in the cinematic surroundings of one of the Western Cape's oldest vineyards in the Stellenbosch wine lands.

More than sixty friends joined us from the UK. It was such a perfect wedding that we all wanted to do it again.

So we did – just two days later. This time James and Vasti, briefly interrupting their honeymoon, were now in the roles of best man and bridesmaid.

On this occasion the venue was another stunning vineyard

just around the mountain and the couple getting married were James' older brother Wesley and Vasti's older sister Wilana.

Two years later the whole group of us from the UK were back once more at the southern tip of Africa for the beachside wedding of my darling daughter Melody to Drikus, the younger brother of Wilana and Vasti. They took their vows looking out to a becalmed sea on a hot and cloudless southern-hemisphere summer's day.

That evening, after I had given my speech as father of the bride and as Melody's beloved chocolate fountain overflowed, I slipped out to a wooden viewing deck for a quiet moment. The moon had perfectly illuminated Table Mountain which towered above me.

In the warm night breeze I reflected on the three marriages that even a fiction writer would hardly have dared to script. Above all, I thought of Carol.

Chapter 1

LONDON, VALENTINE'S DAY 2001

I LOOKED ACROSS THE BED and loved her more than ever. Her softness of manner, her gentle smile and the feel of her olive skin had lost none of their appeal. But above all, what always got to me was the way we could just look into each other's eyes and know we had connected at a level that needed no words.

Our romance began when we were teenagers. Carol was seventeen. I was eighteen, just six months older. She was simply stunning. She had a great figure, long dark hair and sharp fashion sense. Photographs of her testify to this.

I was not remotely in her glamour league. Pictures also testify to this.

Carol did not lack for admirers but by some great mercy, it was me she wanted to go out with. Apparently I could always make her laugh. And so began a truly idyllic few years of courtship.

What Carol did not tell me at the time was that from the beginning she had known that she would one day marry me.

Carol was very down to earth and easy to talk to. She was in London training to be a home economics teacher. I was working shifts of eleven days out of every fourteen as a trainee journalist on a local paper, the *Slough Observer*.

I was impressed at Carol's enthusiasm for her often difficult training and her willingness to volunteer holiday time to spend with kids from deprived backgrounds. On occasion I saw her easy rapport with them.

She in turn would enjoy listening to my various insights into life as a budding reporter as I progressed from covering weddings, funerals and obscure parish councils to murder hunts, celebrity interviews, local and national politics and finally, feature and leader writing on a West London evening newspaper.

Sometimes, as a poorly paid apprentice hack, I would receive great bounty from the news editor in the form of free tickets to cover a dinner-dance at an expensive venue. So for the price of a few minutes of reporting, I was able to take Carol on some impressive dates. I can well remember taking her in my arms at a well-appointed restaurant beside the Thames, surrounded by music and fairy lights, and thinking, "It doesn't get much better than this!"

But it did. We would meet whenever we could, at our family homes, for walks, talks, drives and meals in Burnham Beeches, Windsor, Henley and London. We enjoyed carefree holidays with friends touring Europe.

One sunny summer's day by the Serpentine in London's Hyde Park, we talked of our love and dreams for the future. A few months later it was official, as we got engaged by Eton Bridge with only swans for company.

We were married on 8 December 1973 – five days after Carol's twenty-third birthday. Carol's Dad, an ex-Grenadier Guardsman, proudly gave her away. My Dad, the senior pastor of our local church, married us. He had a twinkle in his eye.

I'll never forget turning to face Carol as she walked down the aisle, more beautiful than I had ever seen her. We looked at each other, smiled and then shared the hymn-sheet. The closeness we both felt at that moment was well expressed in the words we were singing: "Love divine, all loves excelling, Joy of heaven, to earth come down."[2]

Dad took us through our vows. He had conducted countless weddings but he must have been nervous. I still have his minister's manual, which contains the names of his eldest son and soon-to-be daughter-in-law which he had written out in pencil in case he forgot!

He broke up the vows into bite-sized chunks for us to repeat after him. Holding Carol's right hand, I called upon all persons present to witness that I was taking her to be:

> *my lawful wedded wife,*
> *to have and to hold*
> *from this day forward,*
> *for better, for worse,*
> *for richer, for poorer,*
> *in sickness and in health,*
> *to love and to cherish*
> *till death us do part…*

Carol simply looked so happy and secure as I pledged my lifelong commitment to her throughout all eventualities. I somehow held it together as she pledged her lifelong commitment to me.

Our new life as Mr and Mrs began with lots of fun and laughter at a reception with family and friends at a country-house-style conference centre in Burnham Beeches.

This was followed by a honeymoon at "a secret destination", as we budding reporters used to write as we ploughed through the countless wedding announcements that were sent to our office. This usually meant simply that we had no clue where the honeymoon destination was and that we were not inclined

2   Charles Wesley (1707–1788).

to find out. In our case it meant we only travelled as far as Bournemouth on the south coast of England, owing to a petrol crisis at the time.

The hotel that had been recommended to us had a culture as formal as an early 1900s Cunard cruise liner. Our arrival must have brought the average age down by at least half a century. So, naturally, we felt that the only plan of action was to stay in our room for most of the honeymoon. As you do.

Our first home was a new two-bedroom apartment in Slough, which despite all the received wisdom of Sir John Betjeman, Ricky Gervais and many others, actually has its attractions – the Adelphi bingo hall (the Beatles played there!), the chocolate-scented air around the Mars factory, the historic Uxbridge Road gasworks, to mention but a few.

As it happened, it would have been a great loss if the Poet Laureate's "friendly bombs" had fallen on Slough. The greatest attraction for me about the town was always the people, drawn from over ninety ethnic groups. Best of all, Carol was there, our families were there, many of our friends were there and our church was there.

Our church was well known in the town and further afield. It was started by my Dad, known by his initials, W. T. H., or to press and friends as Billy Richards. He was a former coal miner from South Wales who first went down the pits aged fourteen. He worked long shifts "half a mile down and three miles in" six days a week until he was twenty.

He had a strong conversion experience in the hymn-singing valleys of nonconformist Christianity. He came to England convinced God had called him to preach. As he did not have the means or the opportunity to undergo a formal theological education, he relied on the Acts of the Apostles as his guidebook to what church should be like.

Many years later, as a result of following this guidebook, he would be asked to speak to large numbers of clergy and ministers who, he said, half seriously, had more letters after their names than he had in his name.

He was just twenty-seven when he held his first services in a leaky, run-down Scout hut a mile from the centre of Slough. There were just five original members, one of whom, the pianist Marian, became his wife and subsequently mother to me and my younger brother John.

Against post-World War II trends, the church grew, with several hundred people attending weekly services. There was a large group of young people who ran more than twenty-five "branch" Sunday schools and children's and youth clubs that drew a thousand children a week in hired halls around the town.

Annual outings to the coast required a fleet of coaches and, on one occasion, the chartering of an entire train to Barry Island, South Wales, a place which my Dad had thought of as the ultimate travel destination when he was a schoolboy living all of thirty or so miles away.

The strong and enduring church community which Dad and Mum pioneered attracted many who had little or no religious background – people like Carol, who one day invited herself along, having heard two school friends enthusiastically discussing the church.

At a personal level, as we began married life and started moving up in our careers, Carol and I were both grateful for the sincere Christian example, the positive and practical teachings, and most of all the love, of Dad and Mum. They didn't just talk the talk; they really did walk the walk. This was something that had made a big impression on me in my teens as I weighed the arguments for and against Christianity in the development of my own faith.

We would often pop in to see Dad and Mum. One Saturday evening, nine months into our marriage, we were chatting happily with them when Dad suddenly became ill and we had to call the emergency services. As the ambulance men carried him away, he told me, "I'll see you in the morning."

Less than two hours later, Mum, Carol and I were called into a side room of the local hospital to be told that Dad had suffered a massive and fatal heart attack. He was fifty-eight.

The shock to our family, our church family and many friends around the world was considerable. We took calls from far and wide, but people still found the news hard to believe, even when it was announced on a BBC religious broadcast.

The funeral was packed. The local papers paid special tributes to the passing of "Slough's Billy Graham". Then we all had to face a future without a much-loved husband, father and pastor. Carol's gentle comfort was a rock of support through all this, and her wisdom was pivotal in helping me come to a major decision.

Some months after Dad's death, Eric Lavender, the pastor who succeeded him, told me that the church leaders felt I should come and work full time at the church to run its literature and youth ministry. This was not a suggestion which met with my instant approval. Like the biblical prophet Jonah, I wanted to run away from this prospective new calling, and like him – albeit, thankfully, in less extreme circumstances – I experienced a storm of emotions.

For sure, my Dad's death had made me assess at a new level what life was all about and what really mattered. I found myself comparing the temporary nature of journalism with the far-reaching influence of a life given in the service of God and others, as my Dad's had been.

On the other hand, I thought that Christians for too long had avoided journalism, a profession not noted for its piety.

Also, undoubtedly the journalistic life had got into my blood and I was not about to leave it for sentimental reasons.

I asked Carol to help me consider the various pros and cons – vocational, spiritual, financial and personal. Uncharacteristically, she refused, insisting with trademark directness that it was my decision. "Wes, I'm going to bed. You stay up and wrestle with God. Goodnight!"

Within a week, after some major heart-searching, I had made my decision. When I told Carol she seemed amused, never having doubted the outcome of the wrestling match. "I always knew I was marrying a pastor, not a journalist," she said in a matter-of-fact way. And so we started out on a new and winding path of Christian ministry, with all its public and private blessings and challenges.

At first, as Carol was still teaching and head of a department, her support was more personal, although we frequently met people together at our home. Later she would take a more public role, mentoring others and speaking. She listened patiently to my early attempts at preaching and was quick to question any church traditions that seemed to have neither biblical nor contemporary relevance. Her sharp but positive private critiques were to prove a blessing to the congregation.

Church life was rarely dull. I experienced as many, or more, real-life situations as I had in journalism, as people confided their secrets, fears and hopes. I was kept busy with constant pastoral interaction, preaching and teaching, and with new ventures and projects.

One of these involved Carol and I starting a new church in Windsor with one other couple, a small group of friends and the support of the Slough church. Within three years the church had grown to over 250 people. Among these were a number of people who were homeless. Clearly, we had to do something.

At first we temporarily took as many people as we could into our own homes, but a bigger and more permanent solution was needed. We found a very run-down twenty-three-bedroomed old mansion, not far from the Long Walk near Windsor Castle. Carol was right with me in signing to buy the building, although at that point we only had a deposit. She was well aware that if we didn't raise enough funds within six weeks we, and fellow leaders Mark and Rhoda Healey, would have to sell our own homes, and that we would be among the first residents. But amazingly, and with some very focused prayer, we received the funds by the due date via generous giving from the church, fundraising and a loan.

Some time later we were also able to purchase the next-door property from the Crown Estates. Over the next decade and a half we were able to house over 600 families.

Our church had both a local and a global vision. My grandfather, a former trade union leader and lay preacher, told my Dad as a youngster that what would come from their little village church in Wales would one day extend across the globe.

John Wesley, the Methodist pioneer after whom my brother and I had been named, once said, "The world is my parish." It well summed up our church's DNA. So, increasingly, we were involved in overseas ministry in a number of countries, supporting leaders, churches and development projects.

Our own home life was contented and our family grew with the arrival of Wesley, then James two years later, and Melody four years after James. For their early years in particular, we both agreed that Carol should be home based, and even in later years she was always home focused.

As the children grew, Carol was able to travel with me. She was with me on a particularly moving trip to Russia. She visited an orphanage in Moscow where the children clamoured to cuddle her and her fellow visitors.

She spent personal time with Russian women who were distressed by their lifestyles of abuse and multiple abortions. On one occasion, in a large former Olympic gymnastic hall, long lines of people queued up to be prayed for by Carol as they recognized a compassionate touch that transcended language and cultural barriers.

Carol was also a comfort to me and our family when my mother died of cancer, aged sixty-nine. Carol's combination of strength of character, sensitivity to people and enduring feminine appeal made me constantly grateful that we had taken our marriage vows.

We celebrated our twenty-fifth wedding anniversary in some style in Barbados. We didn't really have the money to do so, but it was fun seeing it all come together. First, we had a gift from Carol's parents. Then a contact of a friend, a London diamond dealer, gave me a sizeable discount. Next, James was amused when I asked if he could help me out by giving me temporary access to his student loan. For a while afterwards he kept loyally silent when his Mum later quizzed him on how he had got through it so fast. And finally, with complimentary airline return upgrades to business class when we were at the departure gate, we lived a dream.

The special ring I had bought her fitted perfectly. "Wow, you got it right, Wes!" Carol said, eyes sparkling to match the ring and no doubt satisfied that her years of trying to train me up as a husband had not been entirely wasted.

The actual anniversary meal at The Cliff restaurant was spent overlooking the azure waters of the Caribbean. We were lovers in paradise.

This second honeymoon, an undoubted step up from the

first, seemed to point to a new season of time together, both in ministry and family life.

We were later able to fulfil a long-time goal of touring New England in the fall (as the Americans call autumn) and to witness the wondrous kaleidoscope of trees and multicoloured leaves. We whiled away the hours, content to just be with each other, doing the simple things: walking in woods, looking at the white clapboard houses, chatting in restaurants, relaxing by log fires and, inevitably, visiting antique shops and bookstores.

A return visit gave us a chance to explore Boston's historic sites, to chill out for a few days at Cape Cod and to spend some time in the mountains of New Hampshire with our long-time American friends, Mike and Linda Peters of St Louis.

We had so many laughs, especially when we decided to go moose hunting, not with guns but in our car. Every evening we would go out looking to find at least one of New Hampshire's celebrated moose, but we could never find one. Pete, as Mike was known, concluded that there were no moose: it was just a tourist-board ruse to attract people like us to such an out-of-the-way state.

One of my ambitions was to hike up a reasonable-sized mountain at the ski resort where we were staying out of season. Carol was feeling tired but wanted me to "go for it". So I did, early one Sunday morning, leaving her in the company of Pete and Linda, who agreed to meet me at the top, having taken the cable car.

I hadn't ascended far along a deserted track when I heard noises in the woods at a height taller than my own. Suddenly remembering that I was in an area where bears sometimes roamed, I covered ground up those foothills at a speed that I had never before achieved, and almost certainly will never again equal.

Finally, I came out into a clearing and scampered up

the first ascent. This turned out to be the black run, which inevitably got steeper and steeper. I stopped for breath but also I sensed something more going on. Out of nowhere, I had an experience that felt like a premonition. The thought came into my head: "Remember this moment. Remember this sight." Maybe the thought of close contact with bears had made me aware of mortality, but this didn't seem to fully explain what I was thinking. So I framed the moment in my mind.

I looked down to the beautiful valley below. I could see I had come a long way up the mountain. I turned around and looked up at an increasingly tough ascent. It would be a battle to move forward from here. There was no way back and no easy way forward. But I had to go on. These thoughts stayed in my mind as I struggled slowly upwards and finally made it to the mountain-top.

Carol and Pete and Linda and I celebrated the moment. We stood in awe, gazing at the most incredible vistas that stretched out as far as the eye could see on a cloudless day.

But clouds of another sort began to gather within two months of our return home. By December of the first year of the new millennium, Carol began feeling excessively tired. She developed a dry cough and a disconcerting wheeze. She also started to lose weight.

Over the first few weeks of the New Year she had a series of tests to see what was wrong. An initial bronchoscopy showed no problems. A course of antibiotics proved temporarily helpful. But Carol was still in some discomfort and there was no explanation for the accelerating weight loss.

So on Valentine's Day 2001 Carol was admitted to Hammersmith Hospital in London for more intensive investigation. There would be no celebratory meal. She was unable to eat much and was tiring quickly.

As she lay weakly in her hospital bed, I told her once more how much I loved her. She looked at me and nodded. I don't think she trusted herself to speak at that moment. She took my hand and squeezed it.

I briefly prayed for her, kissed her lightly and let her sleep. I left her with a heavy sense of foreboding – for Carol, for myself, and for three very apprehensive kids.

Chapter 2

FUN AND FAMILY LIFE

THE KIDS HAD ALWAYS BEEN close with us and with one another. Even their birthdays were close. They were all born in September, giving rise to advice from a midwife after our third arrival that in future I should take my wife out on New Year's Eve.

The family stayed close even though by early 2001 our "babies" had grown up. Wesley was now twenty-three and had gone on from his undergraduate degree in economics to gain a Master's degree in development studies at the London School of Economics. He was now planning for a year out in Argentina to improve his Spanish and do some practical field work in development.

Wes had always had big dreams and a big heart to go with them. I remember him saying as a young boy, "When I am older I want to make a lot of money and help a lot of poor people."

James, our second child, had always been a relaxed character who could usually reduce his Mum to laughter, whenever she tried to discipline him, by affecting a look of wounded innocence. But for all his sense of fun, he worked hard when he needed to.

He had followed in his brother's successful footsteps all the way through school. Now, having recently celebrated his twenty-first birthday, he was at the nearby Royal Holloway

University of London campus and was heading into his second-year economics exams.

Melody, our baby girl with her mop of blonde hair, had always been a character and a strong leader. From an early age she referred to her big brothers as "my boys" and could hold her own in their company. But she was also very sensitive to people and would even give up her beloved chocolate to raise funds for the underprivileged.

It was hard to believe that she had so quickly turned into a beautiful young woman and was now, at seventeen, eagerly preparing herself for the future. She had done very well in her GCSEs at the Windsor Girls' School and had now transferred to the sixth form of Kendrick Grammar School in Reading for her A Levels.

Our three children had always been a major focus of our lives. Carol took a break from teaching for their earlier years and delighted in being there for them. As a pastor or shepherd of people, I had long believed that my first flock was in my home.

While we did our best to help them in any way that we could, we also learned much from these three very different characters. As the years passed I reflected that the kids, on balance, had brought us up quite well.

All through the school years our home was a hub for the kids and their friends, and nothing changed when they grew up and went to "Uni". When Wes went to LSE he fitted easily into the role of goodwill ambassador to his circle of international friends, who visited and revisited our family home outside London.

Our dining room frequently rang with laughter and a babble of languages as a mini United Nations group (indeed, some of them would later work for the UN) made the most of the hospitality, wide-ranging discussions and family atmosphere. Carol was adopted by our visitors as their English Mum. I was christened "Papa Wes". The kids became friends with one another's friends.

James, thanks to the proximity of his university, would regularly pitch up with a bunch of hungry mates who, as often as not, would come bearing gifts of laundry, which were in clear need of urgent attention, if not fumigation. On arrival James would smile sweetly at Carol. She would invariably melt. And so our utility room would fill and our refrigerator would empty.

Carol loved every minute of it and made everyone feel welcome. Her skills as a home economist came into full and much-appreciated use.

Melody had a great gift for including people in various events, especially her birthday parties. She was expert in negotiating, always in an upward direction, the number of people that she could invite. Usually this involved an initial appeal to me, who she clearly and not altogether inaccurately regarded as the softer touch. I then had to help her persuade her Mum, who felt that maybe the time had come to scale down on the parties.

On one occasion, with Mel convinced that even cool teenage school friends were still kids at heart, she persuaded us to hire a bouncy castle, for "around fifteen" friends. In the event I recall Carol just rolling her eyes as "around fifty" supposedly sophisticated teenagers had the time of their lives jumping up and down. Years later, pictures of this event are proudly displayed on the Facebook sites of Mel's friends.

It was entertaining and inspirational to watch the kids develop at each stage of their lives. There was never a time when I did not feel privileged to be their Dad. Carol revelled in being a Mum to them. From early days we established a pattern of family meals together, and it had to be a big pastoral crisis to keep me away from them.

The evening meal, particularly, was accompanied by a buzz of conversation and proved a natural opportunity to develop family communication. Sometimes I felt like a traffic cop at an especially busy intersection as we directed the kids in the art of listening as well as speaking: "OK, OK, now listen a minute to what your brother/sister has to say!"

Carol cooked good food but, no doubt like countless other Mums, she had an uphill battle to get them to eat healthy food. Chips were rationed to once a week, complete with their favourite turkey burgers, which were invariably covered in lashings of ketchup. Kids!

Home was a relaxing place for all of us and the kids, despite the occasional territorial disputes, were happy just hanging out with one another and Mum and Dad and family and friends.

They were experts at delaying the moment of bedtime so that they could stay up as long as possible to talk and listen to the variety of visitors that we entertained.

For much of their time at school, Carol and I juggled second careers as their taxi drivers. I would normally take them to school and she would pick them up. Coming home from school, the kids would drop their bags, raid the fridge and unwind with Carol as they watched *Neighbours*, which in those days starred the emerging Kylie Minogue. Years later my stock went up with them when I organized a break during a busy speaking trip in Australia to take Carol and Mel to Ramsay Street in Melbourne, where the popular soap opera was filmed.

Carol had a great ability to keep closely in touch with what each of the kids were up to. She always made a point of telling them, "You can always talk to us about anything." I always made the most of each opportunity for a chat even if it was just popping out for a few minutes with one of them for some local errands.

We talked naturally about everything as they progressed through each stage of childhood and youth: school, teachers, sport, friends, bullying, self-esteem, ambitions, sex, relationships, money, TV programmes, music, the importance of keeping positive attitudes and the core Bible teachings of loving the Lord "with all your heart and with all your soul and with all your strength" and treating others in the way you would like to be treated.

Every day we would pray a brief blessing over each of the kids and encourage them to confidently face, with faith and determination, every challenge they would encounter. As they went through school the kids increasingly came to value this Christian family lifestyle.

Family prayer together was something they had grown up with from their earliest years. So too were basic ground-rules such as no strops or sulks, and sorting out any issues as they arose. As adults they were often to say that Christianity had never been imposed upon them. It was a lifestyle that they experienced and enjoyed.

Outside the home, shopping was a favoured pursuit. Mel recalls long spells in changing rooms laughing as she and Carol tried on dresses and not quitting on their mission until they found what they were looking for. Then, having depleted their finances, they would come home and proudly open up their shopping bags to announce how much money they had saved.

Carol had an unerring ability to accurately "scan" a shop and confidently decree whether or not it contained anything of interest, without even needing to go in. I never did fathom how she did this, nor how parking spaces would open up for her just as she needed one.

At weekends, when the children were younger, we went out as much as we could for drives and walks. The great outdoors was not far away and the open spaces of Windsor Great Park made an ideal setting for picnics and exploration.

As they got older, weekends required almost military planning as the kids tried a variety of sports. Mel played netball for her school and took up gymnastics, swimming, horse-riding and cross-country running. I remember her on one particularly foggy morning suddenly appearing out of the mist and doggedly pushing to the finishing line after others had either finished or given up.

She also had piano lessons, which, along with her brothers, she was not to follow through with – just as I had, regrettably, done before them. The sound of music could be clearly heard, however, as Wes frequently shattered domestic tranquillity with his trumpet practice.

The boys tried baseball, judo, athletics, rugby and soccer. We spent many a wet and windy day on school fields. Wes well remembers my touchline instructions when he replaced an injured goalkeeper in a tense junior football match.

Seeing an opposing forward rush at him on a through ball, I shouted, "Come out, Wes, come out!" He obediently followed his father's instructions, only to watch the ball being lobbed over his head into the now empty goal. "Go back, Wes, go back!" Parents!

I appreciated being let off with only a rueful smile but I need not have worried, for Wes's chances of sporting success lay in another direction. He took up rowing – sculling, actually. He soon went from the Windsor Boys' School D crew to A crew, beginning a career that was to take him to several gold medals in national championships.

His rowing career then went from strength to strength. But he had to overcome his fair share of setbacks. Once he made it to the final camp for selection to the junior Great Britain rowing team. But he was one of just three boys to miss the final cut. His coach, Chris Morrell, something of a legend in rowing circles, drove him home.

On arrival, we could see how hard Wes had taken this setback. So, that evening, he and I went out for a walk and sat for a long time throwing stones into a nearby lake. I thought it best to say little and let him talk. On the way back I told him that the evening had been a time to work through his disappointment. Tomorrow I would ask him for his attitude and plan for the future. Where would he go from here?

In the morning he was up early and was much brighter. "There's still an outside chance I can get in if I enter a race that's coming up and I do well," he said. "I'm going for it!" So he did, and ended up getting the last place in the national squad.

Before retiring at 22 to concentrate on his academic studies, Wes had represented England and later Great Britain at under-16, under-18 and under-23 levels. He also rowed for the University of London. He raced at many venues around the UK and in France, Belgium, Germany and Greece. We had a lot of fun being part of his travelling fan club.

We had talked with James about the challenges of being compared with his older brother if he went to the same school. James saw no reason to go anywhere else and promptly followed up on his brother's successes. He too won several national gold medals and also rowed for Great Britain at under-16 and under-18.

He decided to retire early on entering university, though not before rowing for charity across the English Channel with his friends. A computer printout showed that due to their miscalculation of the tides, they had actually rowed the equivalent of a double crossing. When they finally made it to Dover with darkness having long since fallen, I remember James temporarily walking bow-legged. He did not want to sit down for some while afterwards. Caring father that I was, I couldn't stop laughing.

The boys' rowing feats also took us as a family to innumerable riversides and rowing lakes. All this provided many opportunities for us to relax together as a family and with the kids' friends and their families. Rather than see the boys' activities take them away from us, we decided to do all we could to support them as a family. I became chairman of the school boat club and worked with other parents to raise funds for new boats and make sure all the boys were properly supported and transported to their races.

Mel was a vociferous supporter of her brothers and ran or perched on the front of my bike as we cheered them on from various riverbanks or tracks. Carol usually preferred to conserve her energy, and her poise, by positioning herself with other parents by the finish line. But when the occasion demanded it, and befitting her background as a teacher, she could make herself heard more than any of us.

Such a time was when Wes's crew had made it to the final of the Fawley Challenge Cup at Henley Royal Regatta, the world's oldest regatta which draws crowds of 100,000 people. Ancient tradition in the Steward's Enclosure dictates that no one moves after a race has started. However, Carol, sitting high up in a stand, grew restless when it was announced that the Windsor boat was a length behind.

The next I knew, she had outflanked a shocked official who obviously had thought better than to belatedly stop this determined, attractive woman rushing by in all her finery. Within moments she was at the riverbank, instructing some very polite and very well-dressed spectators that they were to shout for Windsor. "My son is in the Windsor boat," she informed them with infectious maternal enthusiasm.

After apologizing to various officials, I joined this newfound band of supporters whom Carol was by now leading in impressively impassioned chants of "Windsor! Windsor!" The cheering soon turned to exuberant celebration when stroke-man Mark Hunter (later to win Olympic gold) edged the Windsor crew into a decisive lead in the last 200 metres.

Carol's delight, and mine of course, when Wes's crew won, was a joy to behold, as it was two years later when James's crew won in circumstances of almost identical tension, only this time with us stationed by the river from the start.

Holidays were also a time of great memories. In France the kids loved roaming round a fourteenth-century chateau owned by a partner church for their youth ministry. The kids' French did not improve as much as it could have. They confined themselves mainly to such complexities as "*Le ketchup, s'il vous plaît*" when ordering their inevitable *steak frites*, normal dietary rules being temporarily suspended.

As we had friends in America, we were able to sample not only the well-known attractions but also lesser-explored areas such as the Blue Ridge Mountains, the "Lazy River" in Crestwood, St Louis (where we drifted for hours on large rubber rings), and the cowboy Hill Country outside San Antonio, Texas. Here the men of the family accepted the challenge of eating a particularly squishy local delicacy known as Rocky Mountain Oysters. Don't ask!

For her part, Carol rejoiced in catching more fish than any of us at a local lake. She was not altogether humble about it.

The big cities were also times of discovery as we mapped out our own itineraries and hired cars or vans. One self-devised road trip took us straight from the airport into the chaos of New York traffic and the magic of a summer sunset in Manhattan. The kids loved it. We were probably part of only a small number of visitors to attempt to drive around Times Square. The kids egged me on to out-manoeuvre all the yellow taxi cabs, as Carol turned a similar colour.

Visits to Florida's theme parks were times of sheer, simple, exuberant fun, marred only by the disgrace of their father falling into the notorious tourist trap of mislaying the hire car in Pluto or some such sprawling Disney parking lot.

Carol discovered new reserves of energy as she briskly led the way to Space Mountain, the Big Thunder Mountain Railroad and, one of her favourites, Pirates of the Caribbean. It was a delight to see her in such good health, blooming in the sun with her family.

Yet the kids and I remembered that the holidays were not always carefree. On one more recent trip they went very quiet as they realized their Mum could not hike back up a mountain trail that we had all so easily descended. We took it in turns to help pull her up. The kids were subdued as they saw their Mum struggle. However, she quickly recovered and all of us got on with life as usual.

At the close of 2000, however, the kids watched with mounting concern as Carol began losing weight. Something was clearly wrong, but just how sick was their Mum?

As they awaited the results of various tests they had to somehow live with the tension of not knowing what was going on. And now, with Mum no longer at home with them and with Dad out visiting her on Valentine's Day, they quickly tried to rearrange their lives around the events unfolding in one of London's main teaching hospitals.

Chapter 3

DARK DAYS AT HAMMERSMITH

HAMMERSMITH HOSPITAL should have been an easy forty-minute trip from our home. Instead it often took more than double that time, as London traffic slowed stressfully to a virtual standstill. It was a journey that I was to make twice every day for a month that was almost unremittingly grim.

The hospital itself was an impersonal, sprawling labyrinth of buildings, both ancient and modern. It was situated in a graffiti-decorated road, near to boarded-up shops and next door to the dispiriting Victorian spectacle of Wormwood Scrubs Prison. The Scrubs, with its long and troubled history of disturbances and riots, had been described as "a penal dustbin" by a former governor.

As if driving to the hospital was not depressing enough, the winter weather was frequently stormy with gusting winds, torrential rains and dark skies. It was the kind of turbulence that my old grandma Lucy used to say would herald the end of the world.

Certainly, it felt like our future as a family was teetering on the verge of calamity. For Carol and me in particular, it was like a distant nightmare had suddenly returned to haunt us. Fourteen years before, Carol had very nearly died in Hammersmith Hospital. At the time Wes was nine, James was seven and Mel was only three.

I clearly remembered taking a phone call, just as I was about to leave for a couple of hours at Wes's school sports day. A consultant was on the line to say that I needed to come to the hospital urgently. I tried to make sense of the words I was hearing.

"Are you telling me that my wife may die shortly?" I asked.

"That is exactly what I am telling you," came the quiet reply.

Carol had unaccountably started to lose weight and had been admitted to Hammersmith Hospital. Despite tests, doctors failed to explain or halt her weight loss.

As weeks passed her condition grew more serious and complications set in. At various times she contracted pneumonia, pleurisy and developed a blood clot. As soon as one threat was contained, another emerged. There seemed to be multiple threats to her life, as if some malign conspiracy was at work.

The boys, more than Mel, began to understand that their Mum was now very sick, but they couldn't grasp how critical her condition was becoming.

As I faced the prospect of becoming a widower with three young children, I felt too numb to pray much, though many were praying for us. Each night, however, when the kids were finally asleep and family and friends had left, I lay flat out and often exhausted on the lounge carpet with a little Bible open before me.

And each night I read the same passage from Psalm 34 written by King David when his life was in danger. Two verses caught my attention and I kept focusing on them. Verses 6 and 7 said: "This poor man called, and the Lord heard him; he saved him out of all his troubles. The angel of the Lord encamps around those who fear him, and he delivers them."

Somehow I knew we would be delivered. I did not know

how it would happen but I felt sure that the siege would be lifted. Carol would not die, even though the facts increasingly suggested otherwise. Her weight had dropped from around eight and a half stones (54 kg) to just over six stones (38 kg). She was just thirty-six but looked like a very frail old lady.

So I was shocked but not altogether surprised when the consultant called to say that Carol did not have long to live. I rushed to the hospital. But somehow Carol held on.

An African friend, Michael Kolisang, an associate of the German evangelist Reinhard Bonnke, heard of the crisis and called to ask if he could come with me to the hospital. He wanted to anoint Carol with oil and lay hands on her head, in accordance with biblical direction on healing. And that is what he did, having quickly gathered some olive oil from our kitchen.

That night, whether by coincidence or, as I believed, as an immediate answer to prayer, Carol slept soundly for the first time in many weeks. Very shortly afterwards doctors told us that they had diagnosed what was wrong. The news was serious but hopeful.

Carol had a rare chronic autoimmune disease called scleroderma, meaning "thick skin". In essence the immune system malfunctions and attacks the body instead of protecting it.

Scleroderma causes the skin to thicken and tighten and changes other connective tissues such as tendons, joints, ligaments and the capsules around vital organs that hold a body together. More worryingly, we learned that scleroderma can affect internal organs such as the heart, lungs and kidneys.

The bad news was that no one knew what caused scleroderma, nor was there a cure. The better news, however, was that the disease could be managed.

From this point on Carol slowly began to recover and was

subsequently discharged from hospital. At first the doctors wanted to see Carol every three months. But as she improved, check-ups were extended to every six months, and then every nine months.

Carol was back to living a relatively normal life. Sometimes she would get out of breath on walks that others managed easily. She needed to have a good night's rest but she was still well able to cope with the occasional late night out. Mostly she was very active.

Over the next decade few people meeting Carol for the first time would have guessed that there was anything amiss. There was, however, always the chance of recurring serious illness.

We did not make a big thing of it with the kids, although they knew their Mum was prone to sickness. Nor did we live in dread of what could be. But now in the winter months of 2001, here we were back at Hammersmith, and things were once more looking ominous.

Just to look at Carol was to witness that there was something seriously wrong. Her weight continued to drop alarmingly. Within eleven weeks she had lost over 6.4 kg in weight and was now down to 51 kg.

At the same time she lost her appetite. She was short of breath and would have sudden stabbing pains when she moved. She rarely groaned and never moaned. But her face was frequently a picture of acute discomfort.

The doctors took quick action to try to deal with the initial pain, although it was not pretty to watch. A day after her admission the doctors cut what seemed to my amateur eyes a gruesomely large hole in Carol's left side to insert a tube known as a chest drain. In this very basic way excess fluid was drawn off the upper part of Carol's chest.

Initially one and a half litres of fluid were drained from Carol, with more to follow subsequently. I was startled by the amount. No wonder she had been in such discomfort. Not surprisingly, she was feeling very much better a day or two later.

The drain was soon removed and the stitches later came out well. Having navigated one immediate danger, the next pressing matter was the need to halt Carol's weight loss. At the best of times managing Carol's diet could be a challenge.

She was a coeliac, so needed to avoid any food containing wheat. This ruled out a big range of everyday food that most people take for granted – bread, cakes, crackers, cheeses, sauces, seasonings and many drinks. Shopping involved a lot of detective work in checking labels to ensure that Carol would not inadvertently eat "wheat-contaminated" food that would make her ill.

Some of the gluten-free products on offer at the time, such as bread that resembled cardboard, were unappetising to say the least. Now she had reached a point where she didn't feel like eating at all and the overcooked hospital food on offer did nothing to help matters. The sachets of instant food recommended by the dieticians were equally unappealing.

"I'm sorry, Wes, I just can't eat this stuff," said Carol with the concerned look of a professional who needed no telling how important it was to eat properly.

With a feeling of quiet desperation, I did my own shopping and brought in food that was more enticing. I cut it up into small portions and tried to make it look presentable. But despite her best efforts, Carol could only manage to eat pitifully small portions. Her appetite took an agonizingly long time to return.

It was not the only development that seemed slow to me. The days passed without any news of what was wrong with Carol. Even though I knew that accurate diagnosis, which required thorough investigation, was the key to effective treatment, the suspense of being in no-man's-land was hard to live with.

The first days of her stay in hospital were a time of doctors coming and going, multiple biopsies and all kinds of examinations. Carol had to undergo CT scans, ECGs, X-rays, endoscopies and a visit to the radiologist. Some of these tests meant that she needed to take only fluids – another unfortunate, if necessary, contribution to her weight loss.

Carol, though benefiting from the chest drain, was still very lethargic and needed to be helped to the toilet. She also needed oxygen and a blood transfusion to get her stabilized.

She was regularly put in a wheelchair and taken for test after test in various outposts of a very far-flung medical empire. The wear and tear of simply turning up at the right place at the right time and waiting in line was taking a toll on Carol.

On occasions when she was too weak to even get into a wheelchair, she was moved in her bed along draughty corridors that seemed designed to invite the winter cold. I walked briskly alongside the hospital porter, doing what pitifully little I could to readjust her blankets wherever necessary to keep her warm.

Slowly Carol got into a routine that allowed her to rest and she began to sleep well at night. Her temperature, which needed careful watching, began to settle at acceptable levels.

As a family we developed a routine of our own. Late each morning or early afternoon, depending on my various responsibilities, George Shaw, a friend from church, would come and collect me, to save me the stress of the drive.

George not only took time out every day from his businesses to chauffeur me in his Mercedes to the hospital. He would also often stay with me to keep me company and keep my spirits up – a generous act that was a lifeline to me and which touched all of our family deeply.

Terry Beasley, another church friend since teenage years who had taken early retirement to be my executive assistant

– providentially, as it transpired – was the interface between home and church. He was also part of the rota of guys from the church who made it their business to pick me up each evening. Such support at a time of trouble played a big part in keeping us all going.

Family members and friends came to visit. My brother John and his family travelled up from Cornwall. Ken and Lois Gott, old family friends, made the long trek from the North-East. Steve Chalke, founder of the Oasis Trust, was the most frequent of a number of Christian leaders who came to Hammersmith.

We greatly appreciated all these visits, but mostly we needed to keep things quiet for Carol. The kids came as regularly as they could, while trying to maintain their momentum for their studies. Mel would often get up on the bed with Carol and just lie nestled against her for extended periods.

The boys were trying to cheer their Mum up, but the pain in their eyes was hard to watch. Wes also had a big decision to make. He was due to leave shortly for his year out in Argentina, but he was in no mood to leave his Mum like this.

I talked with a senior doctor and told him that we needed to quickly cancel or go ahead with the visit. "It's best your son doesn't go too far away right now," he said guardedly.

Though we didn't know it at the time, the findings coming back from the labs were beginning to confirm the doctors' worst suspicions. A CT scan had shown "lymph nodes present in the thorax" (the chest) which "may or may not be malignant". Further investigation was necessary. The doctors were understandably cautious at this point about what to share with us.

One junior doctor, however, was less circumspect. In response to my enquiry as to when we could expect any definite news, she confided more than I expected her to and, no doubt, more than her senior colleagues would have sanctioned. Even so, it confirmed what I had suspected.

"We don't think that your wife has got more than three months," she said in a matter-of-fact way, before moving on to join her band of colleagues.

For some moments I just stood there, in a bare hospital corridor, trying to absorb what I had just heard. Could I be sure that the doctors had really reached such a definite conclusion when tests were still continuing? On the other hand, why would the young doctor say such a thing if there was no foundation for it? She may have been inexperienced in how to respond to a question such as I had asked. But I also knew from journalistic experience that "unofficial" leaks, like the one I had just received, were very often highly accurate.

I thought it was best not to say anything to anyone for the moment, especially to Carol and the kids. I tried to convince myself that nothing had really changed and to resist speculating on all the circumstantial evidence. But for sure, it didn't take an expert to see that every day was increasingly a battle for Carol. Also the fact that we had the heads up to cancel Wes's trip seemed to be a clear sign that there was bad news to come. But right now we could only wait for conclusive results of all the tests.

On 1 March, at 8 p.m., Professor Jonathan Waxman knew what he had to say as he entered Carol's hospital room to speak to us both. Professor Waxman, one of the hospital's leading specialists, was kindly but forthright. "We have now completed all our tests. I am afraid that they show conclusively that you have cancer," he told Carol.

The moment I heard these few words, I felt my mouth go dry and my heart start thumping. I thought, *Oh God, no! Not cancer! So the junior doctor was right after all. Carol doesn't have long to live.*

I looked anxiously at Carol. Her face gave little away. She was just listening intently to everything Professor Waxman had to say.

"It's Non-Hodgkin's lymphoma," he continued. This meant nothing to either of us at the time. But Professor Waxman was quick to educate us. He did so in a surprisingly hopeful manner. "There is a high success rate with this kind of cancer. You will need to have chemotherapy and it will not be easy. But we are going to do our best to make this go away." He then gave us some details of future treatment plans, answered a few routine questions and left us alone.

Carol and I just looked at each other. I felt tears welling up but did not cry. Nor did Carol. She just shook her head slowly, let out a deep breath and said quietly, "Wes, I never thought it would come to this."

"Neither did I," I replied. "I knew it was bad, but not this bad."

But I told Carol how heartened I was to hear what Professor Waxman had said about the treatment. "Carol, we've come through so much before. We can do so again."

Carol, ever the fighter, nodded her agreement. "Yes, there's no way I'm giving up." We just gently hugged. And then we prayed – for healing, for strength and for wisdom to share this with the kids.

As they saw my serious face when I returned from Hammersmith Hospital, they guessed that things were pretty bad. I struggled to get out my opening line.

"Kids, I'm really sorry to have to tell you this, but there's no easy way to put it: your Mum has cancer."

They betrayed no immediate reaction but were grim faced as I quickly tried to move on to the more positive words of Professor Waxman. "The news is bad but it's not all bad. The doctors are hopeful of treating it and we can pray that once more, Mum will come through all this."

I reminded them how God had helped us before when they were too little to appreciate the extreme threat to their Mum's health and the future well-being of the family. God had delivered their Mum once before and He was well able to do so again. So we needed to keep peace in our hearts and have faith. I was speaking to myself as much as the three of them.

The kids just stood there for a moment. Wes and James, each tall and athletic and used to racing against tough opposition, looked as vulnerable as when I used to scoop them in my arms as toddlers. Mel just looked lost.

I could hardly bear to look at the kids. But I could not miss their tears that were welling up. I could not hold back my tears either. I wanted to do more to comfort them but all I could do was reach out and pull us into a tight circle. We hugged each other and prayed for a miracle.

Chapter 4

TREATMENT AND REPRIEVE

HE HOPEFUL WORDS of Professor Waxman reminded me of a pilot's reassurance during some particularly bumpy weather. At least we knew that someone in the cockpit was confident that we should not panic. But we also needed to strap in tight for further turbulence up ahead.

Right now every effort needed to be concentrated on preventing Carol's health taking a further nosedive. In the short period while oncologists were deciding on their plan of action, Carol's weight continued to drop. Her poor appetite was compounded with difficulty in swallowing and bouts of diarrhoea. She was now officially "clinically malnourished" and "at risk of further weight loss".

We urgently needed to up her calorie and protein intake. A special diet was ordered by the hospital dietician and I continued to do my daily shop at a specialist food store.

Carol, meanwhile, was very weak and needing a lot of rest. She needed all the strength she could muster for the biggest battle of all – the battle against the malignant B or T cells that were remorselessly causing destruction in her lymph system.

Looking at her, I fretted about her readiness to undergo a gruelling course of chemotherapy, especially as she was in no state to even go to the clinic. But on 7 March a saline (salt water) intravenous drip was brought to her bed and a combination of drugs known as CHOP was injected into her vein.

This was one of the most common chemotherapy regimens for treating Non-Hodgkin's lymphoma. The hope was that, after six cycles of treatment at three-week intervals, all the cancer cells would be killed and all tumours would have shrivelled and disappeared.

Cancer treatment had made huge advances, but there was no knowing how Carol would respond or how she would react to side-effects that, given her medical history, could cause serious complications.

I wished I felt more confident about the outcome. I prayed that I would but I still couldn't get an inner peace. For some reason, I did not have the assurance of fourteen years before that we would be delivered from the threat of losing Carol. This worried me. I was so sure then. I was nowhere near so certain now. Why was that?

Was I having a crisis of faith when faced with the dreaded spectre of cancer? Was I simply too emotionally upset to just focus on God's promise in the Psalms, which, for sure, had not changed with the passage of time? Or did I have no assurance for the simple and stark reason that Carol, and our family, would not be delivered this time around?

I prayed for a passage from the Bible that would speak directly to our situation. One dull morning, while walking routinely into the hospital, and without any quivering sensations or angelic visitations, I received it. Psalm 121, which I knew well, just came into my mind:

> *I lift up my eyes to the hills –*
> *where does my help come from?*
> *My help comes from the Lord,*
> *the Maker of heaven and earth.*

He will not let your foot slip –
he who watches over you will not slumber;
indeed, he who watches over Israel
will neither slumber nor sleep.
The Lord watches over you –
the Lord is your shade at your right hand;
the sun will not harm you by day,
nor the moon by night.
The Lord will keep you from all harm –
he will watch over your life;
the Lord will watch over your coming and going
both now and for evermore.

I could not figure all this out. There weren't many hills around Hammersmith. The nearest high point I could see at that moment was the prison next door. Nor did it seem that Carol had been spared from harm. Yet the core message of the psalm was clear. In all the comings and goings, God Himself was watching over us.

I shared this with Carol, as I was to do many times in the days ahead. She too found considerable reassurance in the psalmist's words. She also had a "word" from Psalm 91 that brought her both comfort and confidence.

Carol was now starting to sleep better and in the days following her treatment she had no notably adverse reactions. Within the week, her appetite was improving and for the first time in weeks she had gained a little weight.

Despite her treatment-induced loss of hair, she was looking altogether much brighter and she was ready to come home. A month after first going to hospital, she was discharged on 13 March.

It was as if all was right with the world again when we had

Carol back in the centre of her domain. The kids visibly relaxed. She let out a big sigh of pleasure when we helped her into her own bed.

She rested a lot over the coming days. Her mood was much brighter and she was eating much better at home.

The next trip to Hammersmith was on 26 March for the second cycle of CHOP. This should have been a reasonably straightforward outpatient visit. Instead it was complicated by the detection of another pulmonary embolus, a potentially life-threatening blood clot in the lung. So Carol started receiving a course of injections with the anticoagulant drug Tinzaparin.

She made light of this setback and even found some amusement in showing off some distinctly non-fashionable white medical tights. "What do you think of these, Wes?!"

By 5 April there was another cause for alarm, as Carol was feeling unwell and feverish. She was running a temperature at around 38.5 degrees centigrade. The doctors wanted her to be readmitted urgently. So we rushed her to the hospital straight away for close monitoring of her temperature and blood count. She had yet another course of intravenous antibiotics. She had developed a chemotherapy-related condition known as "neutropenic sepsis". In short, this meant that any delay in treatment carried a serious risk of rapid deterioration into shock and could prove fatal.

So began yet another wearying spell in hospital for Carol and a discouraging return to the old routine of visits for the family. Slowly, however, her temperature stabilized. Her regular nausea had gone and she had stopped the all-too-frequent vomiting. She was recovering from anaemia after having two blood transfusions. Things were once more looking up.

With Easter approaching, Carol was more than ready to be "sprung" from what now seemed like a medical prison.

George Shaw decided that we should do this in some style. On Good Friday, 13 April, Carol was wheeled to the front entrance of Hammersmith Hospital to be greeted by the impressive sight of a waiting Bentley Arnage Red Label and George, complete with chauffeur's hat, standing to attention. The porter's face was a picture of wonderment as to the identity of his celebrated charge.

Carol hid her surprise well. She just smiled regally at George and stepped out of her wheelchair and into the prestigious car as if she had been doing this all her life. George (whose cap, I noticed, randomly sported a long grey ponytail) then took us on a guided tour around London. We stopped briefly by the Serpentine where we had decided to get married.

George gave us some moments alone when we got out to breathe in the spring air and have a kiss and cuddle. For sure, we had not dreamed all those years ago of what we would face together. But neither could we have imagined back then the depth of love that now held us so close.

A week later, after the big pick-me-up of being home for Easter, Carol was back at Hammersmith for her third CHOP. It was still early in the treatment but already, after two cycles, the doctors were noticing some positive changes in her overall condition.

Each chemotherapy treatment now followed a predictable pattern. We would make the trip to the outpatients' area of Hammersmith's oncology department. For the next few hours Carol would read, chat and have a cup of tea or coffee while the drugs were fed into her. At some point she would see Professor Waxman and arrangements would be made for a further scan.

Then Carol would come home and face an inevitable down period. She had steroid tablets for five days to help lessen the nausea and vomiting. But mostly, for the first week after treatment, she still felt pretty rough and slept a lot. Despite a slight improvement in the week after finishing the steroids, she would usually struggle to do much. Then in the week or so before the next cycle she would dramatically pick up and we would marvel at the turnaround in her energy levels.

By the end of May, two weeks after her fourth cycle, Carol had improved considerably. She had no further infections or complications and was breathing well. She was, however, still finding it difficult to put on weight. She weighed 44.9 kg. But she was well enough and happy enough for Wes to leave for Barcelona, where he signed up for a month's intensive language school as a prelude to several months' work.

By her fifth treatment on 4 June, Carol's weight had increased to 46.2 kg. She was still very lethargic the week after treatment, but there were now no mouth ulcers and no fevers. The best news of all was that she was now able to get out and about for the first time in six months. This she did wearing various funky little hats, having decided a wig was not the way to cover her baldness. Walking slowly with Carol by the nearby River Thames in the summer sun, I felt as if I had just hit the jackpot.

Her last clinic was on 25 June. Her weight was still slowly climbing and was 47.4 kg. She was feeling much better after the dosage of steroids had been reduced. The doctors noted that "her clinical response continues".

The big question hanging over everything was what all the treatments had actually achieved. Was the cancer still there or had it been beaten?

We approached our next meeting with Professor Waxman on 16 July with barely concealed tension. Carol walked unaided and purposefully into the consulting room.

Professor Waxman's mood was as bright as we had known. He spoke carefully but hopefully. Carol's condition was clearly vastly improved from her arrival on Valentine's Day.

"You have coped very well with the treatment," he told her as he pointed out the results of the latest scan. "The CT scan shows that the nodal masses have gone away. Right now you are clear of cancer. I am very pleased with the result, but the next year is the risk period."

Even though Professor Waxman could not say for sure that the cancer had disappeared for good, this was by far the best news we had heard for many a long month. Right now what mattered was that Carol had a future.

Both she and I involuntarily let out huge sighs of relief. I looked at her, and whole layers of apprehension had gone in an instant. She gave me a restrained smile that hinted at a far greater inner excitement. I somehow resisted the urge to envelop her there and then with hugs and kisses.

In truth, I was so happy I could have hugged Professor Waxman as well. Instead, as true Brits, we simply thanked him warmly, received his best wishes and almost weightlessly glided out of his office. We couldn't wait to get home and share the good news with the kids and all our friends and prayer supporters.

We took it quietly over the summer, going out for walks and drives and doing our best to see that Carol was well fed and well rested. She was feeling increasingly encouraged, especially when the kids' exam results came through. Despite all the distractions and uncertainties they had endured, James had achieved a 2:1 in his economics degree and Mel got four As in her first-year A Level exams. Carol told them with a smile, "I wouldn't have expected anything less from you!"

By 4 September there was more good news. A report from the rheumatology clinic said: "This lady is currently very well. Recent CT scan clear. Blood picture is stable."

Four days later, with the excitement and anticipation of

young kids, Carol and I set off for a two-week holiday on the Spanish island of Minorca with George and Carole Shaw. They joked that their mission was "to fatten Carol up". Her weight at the time was 49.1 kg. So the plan was to go out to as many restaurants as we could. They were as good as their word as they took us to candlelit suppers and little-known bistros by the water's edge at lunchtimes. It was light-years away from the gloom of Hammersmith.

A day after our arrival, however, a very different type of gloom descended as we took a call from England, telling us that planes had flown into the World Trade Center in New York. As there was no TV at the villa where we were staying, we quickly made our way to a local bar where we saw scenes that, along with the rest of the world, we could barely comprehend.

We urgently made a number of calls to check on family, church members and friends in America. One church friend, a businessman, had been just a few blocks from Ground Zero but he had got out safely.

Wes, who came over from Barcelona to celebrate his twenty-fourth birthday with us, recalls thinking that "we had been staring death in the face trying to keep Mum alive. Yet here were thousands of people with no sickness who had left for work healthy but who were now gone for ever. It just reinforced how fragile life is and how grateful we were that Mum was still with us, skinny or not. More than ever we needed to maximize every day."

Every morning I framed Carol in my mind as we sat out in the warmth for breakfast and prayers. Every day I thanked God for such simple pleasures as being able once more to just go out hand in hand for a stroll together.

Carol was relishing her increased energy and new-found freedom of movement. As we all chatted on a hilltop overlooking the sparkling waters of the Mediterranean, it was getting easier to believe that maybe, after everything, the good times really were back again.

Carol came home in high spirits and full of plans for Mel's eighteenth birthday on 29 September. She ordered roses, bought her a new outfit and oversaw the transformation of our house and garden into party-land. Mel's friends arrived in even larger numbers than usual and Carol spoke in glowing terms of her baby. She said how much she was looking forward to the two of them going on a "girls' tour" of the UK and Ireland the following year. It was a tonic to see Carol increasingly reconnecting with life.

On Sunday, 7 October 2001, for the first time since Christmas Eve 2000, Carol was back with the church family. As we followed her to the platform, the congregation jumped to their feet. They were cheering and clapping and some were wiping tears away.

Carol looked good, with her close-cropped black hair and wearing a roll-neck jumper and black trousers. She took the microphone, with Mel and I standing beside her and the boys slightly behind. But though she appeared cool, she was not fully composed.

"It's been a long haul and a long time to come to this point," she began in a measured way, clearly battling to control her emotions. "Obviously, we could not have got through it without a lot of support from you all. And, of course, we couldn't have got through it without the Lord."

Carol thanked everyone for their prayers and practical acts of support. She made particular mention of the church's children, for their simplicity of faith in their prayers. "You cannot overestimate the power of prayer and what it has meant to us as a family. It has brought comfort and faith at a very difficult time."

She thanked me and also the church's leadership for releasing me to be with her 24/7. She faltered as she talked of our kids. "This has been the hardest thing for them to go through."

She spoke of the need to stand firm in faith on the promises of the Bible. "When you have got nothing else to hold on to, just stand on the Word. There is nothing else. Right from the beginning the word I had was from Psalm 91, and that came from many people who wrote to me. I think we read that every day for the last ten months. We stood on this word and we believed this word. We continue to stand on it and we continue to believe it, because not everything is dealt with. I ask you to continue to stand with us because there are still a number of things that aren't right and we still need a number of answers."

There was more applause as Carol finished her speech. There were more tears, too, as Maurice Benton, one of the church leaders, led a prayer of thanks "that Carol is here today". It was too much for James, who buried his head on his Mum's shoulders. She turned round immediately and held him in her arms.

Just two weeks later, when everything was apparently going so well, it was Carol who needed to be held in my arms.

Lying in the bath one evening in late October, she routinely checked her breasts for any changes. She stopped as she felt a hard mass in her left breast. Then she let out a piercing scream that chilled me the moment I heard it. I jumped up from the adjoining bedroom and ran to the bathroom. Carol was sobbing more than I had ever seen her sob before. "Wes, it's back. It's back. The cancer has come back!"

I helped her out of the bath and I covered her in a large warm towel. We lay together on our bed as I hugged her tightly. Neither of us said anything. By now Carol had stopped crying. She just went still, almost rigid. I was too stunned to cry or pray.

We were both in shock. Complete and utter, immobilizing shock. We didn't move for some time. It felt like a huge iron ceiling was remorselessly being lowered towards us and that we were about to be crushed.

Chapter 5

BETWEEN A ROCK AND A HARD PLACE

C AROL'S SELF-DIAGNOSIS led to an immediate flurry of medical activity. We were soon back at Hammersmith for a biopsy and CT scans. All attention centred on finding out whether a hard mass of just 3.5 cm was benign or malignant.

The tension of this wait surpassed even the suspense of previous waits. For days we had to get on with life as usual, in the knowledge that every hope of a normal life, which had recently come so tantalizingly into view, could well be on the point of being dashed.

Just when we thought that Carol was once more moving forward, as Winston Churchill once put it, "into broad sunlit uplands", she now could be about to "sink into the abyss" of a new and more sinister darkness.

I barely knew what to do with myself. The kids had a hard time settling at anything. But Carol seemed to have an ability to press the "pause" button as she patiently waited for news that would mark her future for good or ill. At last, on Friday, 9 November 2001, the moment arrived when we were once more in the office of Professor Waxman at Hammersmith.

The last time we had seen him he was the cautious bearer of good news. Now, just a few months after he had explained that the next year would be critical, he was subdued. Carol, as it now became all too clear, had indeed been justified in her worry about the lump in the left breast. Professor Waxman, gravely but gently, explained that cancer had now spread to the breast and the lymph nodes.

Before we could react to this news he added: "But we are not going to give up. I am going to send you to a very special man who trained me at Barts."

"Barts" – St Bartholomew's Hospital in the heart of the City of London – was the famed centre of British medical excellence that was founded in 1102 by Rahere, an outstanding monk who cared for the sick and poor.

It was now one of Britain's leading cancer treatment and cancer research centres. For us it was to become a virtual second home on many occasions over the following eight months.

At first Carol was able to walk briskly through the Henry VIII clock-tower entrance and under The Archway to The Square, a tree-filled oasis of serenity with its cascading fountain in the centre of the hospital wings. As time went on and Carol's condition deteriorated, we would have to push her in a wheelchair where she had so recently walked. Later she would be taken directly by ambulance on a bed and become an inpatient.

On our trips to Barts we were to experience all four seasons – late autumn, winter, spring and summer – but for Carol, medically speaking, the seasons were reversed. Her prognosis grew bleaker as the surrounding scenes grew brighter.

All this was ahead of us when we first met the distinguished Professor Andrew Lister on Thursday, 15 November. Professor Lister, who had then been at Barts for almost thirty years, was Director of the Cancer Research UK Medical Oncology Unit and a Fellow of the Royal College of Physicians, the Royal College of Pathologists, the Royal College of Radiologists and the Academy of Medical Sciences. In short, he was himself something of an institution within an institution.

For all this, he was an immediately reassuring figure – personable and professional, in an understated English way. He was warm towards us but even the apparent small talk had a purpose. His first questions, as Carol was changing for an examination, were aimed to give him a profile of the family. How old was I? How was my health? How old were the kids? What were they doing?

I must have been on autopilot, because only later did it dawn on me that these questions were geared to finding out not only what support his patient would have but also what the situation would be for the family if treatment of his patient was unsuccessful.

Professor Lister explained that he wanted to get the most thorough picture possible of Carol's condition. He would therefore be quickly arranging for her to see a number of his colleagues for examinations and scans. "You are in for a busy week," he said. He was not exaggerating.

We left sobered by the seriousness of the situation. At the same time we felt boosted by the thought that everything that could be done by the medical profession was being done to help Carol. We were cheered to know that some of the best people in the UK were on Carol's case and at no cost to us, amazing as this sounded to our American friends. I remember feeling grateful for the free British National Health Service which meant that financial stress would not be added to our considerable current pressures.

That initial session produced a whirlwind of appointments with various specialists at Barts and several other London hospitals. Some, like the London Hospital opposite the Blind Beggar pub in the Mile End Road (where General William

Booth had visited in the early days of the Salvation Army), were cold, old, depressing, Victorian structures. Others were light and welcoming and bore the signs of major new investment.

Carol showed great patience as we spent hour after hour in waiting rooms. She was content to sit and chat or read a magazine. I found it harder to cope with, but she urged me to "just go with the flow". For sure, I prayed and tried to receive the peace of God, which I knew could "guard my heart and mind". But it was a battle to get the peace and even more of a struggle to keep it.

I was inwardly on edge and found it hard to do nothing, although I did manage the occasional moments when I tried to focus on the goldfish tanks that appeared to be the only lively aspect of hospital waiting rooms. Mostly I felt better when I could just "do something" like going off and getting Carol a coffee or a little snack. The reality was that I knew that real help for Carol was way beyond my ability to deliver.

Getting around and in and out of London with a weak person became a daily challenge. I was glad of all the backup from family and friends – a vital lifeline in times of trouble.

By now Wes had returned from Barcelona, having received a tough phone call from me to say that the cancer was back. Carol had not wanted to ask him to return home but as soon as he came through the front door and gave her a hug, she just wept over him.

Wes's support would once more prove to be invaluable. Each day he or James would help me get Carol up, dressed and prepared. We made sure that she had hat, scarf and heavy coat ready for when she would have to brave the bitingly cold November weather to get to and from the car. George would arrive early and we would settle Carol in the back of his Mercedes with pillows and blanket so she could rest.

Although the uncertainty of that week was considerable, Carol's spirit was remarkably positive. She and I prayed together each day and kept focused on the scriptures that had become so real to us. But it was not all "spiritual stuff". Carol enjoyed some banter, especially when it was at my expense.

Once, when we thought she was sleeping, we had slowed to a virtual stop in central London traffic. Out of the blue she enquired, with mock innocence and probably without opening her eyes, "Have we taken another one of your shortcuts, Wes?" George, who had followed my supposedly inspired hunch to save time, just grinned at me. In my defence, I have to say that at least one in ten of my shortcuts worked.

Hanging over every moment of light relief, however, was the concern that the next meeting with Professor Lister, on 28 November, would be a very heavy one. What had all the tests and scans shown? How advanced was the cancer? Above all, we needed to know whether there was any medical hope of beating it.

We entered the consulting room trying to control our apprehension. We were seated for a few minutes while waiting for Professor Lister's arrival. I tried unsuccessfully to dismiss an image that came to mind, of prisoners in suspense on death row.

Neither Carol nor I said much to each other. We were so close, yet at this moment it seemed hard to speak. Any small talk seemed an intrusion and an irrelevance. We just wanted to get on with this and hear whatever it was that we had to hear.

A young trainee doctor came in, clearly well aware of what news the couple sitting before her were about to hear. She had been particularly kind to us but at this moment she struggled to talk to us. It was not hard to guess why. In her awkwardness, she nervously let slip that this was going to be "a difficult conversation, so we had better wait for Professor Lister."

I could sense her relief, which I shared, when the door

opened and in walked Professor Lister in his trademark white coat. We exchanged brief greetings, and then he came straight to the point. He outlined how the cancer had spread. Urgent decisions on treatment were needed.

His next words to Carol are embedded in my memory: "We have to make this go away or you will go away and this will be your last Christmas."

Professor Lister paused. None of us said anything for a few moments. I turned slowly to look at Carol. She was looking down. The consulting room was suddenly very silent as she and I tried to absorb the news we had just heard.

"What time-frame are we talking about?" I asked quietly. Professor Lister, with the wisdom of someone who had long experience of such difficult conversations, said he could not be exact. I pressed him to be as open with us as he could. "It could be six to nine months," he said.

Again there was silence in the room. I struggled to comprehend these few words that spelt out the clear and present danger of death to a wonderful person, a marriage, a family and a future.

I felt my eyes pricking. My head and my heart were in overdrive. But a survival instinct told me to try to stay focused. There were still big questions to be asked and big decisions to be made.

I squeezed Carol's hand. She looked composed but, even though I knew her so well, I could only guess at the extent of her inner turmoil. She held it together enough to ask questions about possible future courses of treatment, if indeed there were any.

Professor Lister was stark in his appraisal. Carol could choose to immediately undergo treatment more intense than any she had experienced before. This, at best, would leave her very seriously ill. Her immune system would be so weakened that she would have to be kept in a special isolation room. Any infection could be fatal.

I tried to take in all that Professor Lister was saying to us. Was there any alternative at all, Carol wondered?

He spelt it out. "You are between a rock and a hard place. If we do not treat you, then you will die. If we do treat you, there is a high chance the treatment will kill you, as you are so weak. But we can take a punt on the treatment if you wish."

Take a punt. The phrase jarred me. So this was what it had all come down to. A gamble on highly toxic treatment with terminally loaded dice.

Not only that, but with the stakes so high, we had just a few minutes to decide what our next move would be. My mind went into turbo mode on several levels – personal, pastoral and philosophical.

Did we really want to risk Carol ending her days, isolated from her family in a hospital bed, pumped full of chemicals? Would there not be far more dignity in facing up to death at home, where she could be cared for by those who knew and loved her best? And anyway, could she take such treatment? Her body was already ravaged by illness. She had been through so much.

Underlying all these thoughts was my worldview of life and death. For all the expertise of the medical profession, which I greatly valued, did I really believe that they necessarily had the last say on Carol's future? No, I did not. They could only do so much and right now they could guarantee no answers. The medical profession had reached its limits. But with God I believed there were no limits. Anything was still possible. Above all, I believed that our lives and times were in His hands.

Even so, this was a huge decision to make. Were we really ready to turn down Professor Lister's "punt" that at least provided the outside chance of Carol making it through heavy-duty treatment? But all things considered, I thought the "punt" was not an option.

Whatever I might think about it, however, I knew I was not the one who had to make this decision. Although Carol was so much part of me, it was her life and prospective death that we were talking about.

I turned to Carol as Professor Lister waited for our response. She looked at me, pursed her lips and slowly shook her head. There was pain in her eyes as she looked into mine. Then she began to speak quietly. She was poignantly apologetic. She said, "Wes, I'm sorry, but I just can't take any more. I just can't. And I don't think I should take any more treatment. I'm through with treatment."

She looked to me for reassurance. I nodded my agreement and marvelled at the sheer guts of my darling, weakened wife. What a fighter she was! She had been through so many bruising rounds of treatment. She had come through an epic struggle for her life when the kids were young. She had endured all the more recent sicknesses and setbacks of a heavyweight bout of chemotherapy but now, faced with a more daunting challenge than any she had faced before, she had had enough.

My every instinct recoiled against throwing in the towel but there comes a time when even the most bloodied fighter needs to be saved from further punishment. For Carol, medically speaking, that time had arrived.

The key decision made, Professor Lister talked with us about plans for palliative care. He asked Carol if she wished to receive some experimental antibody treatment as part of a clinical trial. Carol agreed to this without pinning her hopes on its effectiveness.

With nothing more to be said, she whispered to me, "Just

take me home, Wes." I thanked Professor Lister for his help, put my arm around Carol and headed out to meet George in the waiting room.

I wanted to give Carol a long hug but I knew that she would want to stay strong. She would not want to break down here in a sterile hospital corridor. So I just held her close, told her I loved her and said a little prayer as we kept on walking. "Lord Jesus, please help us. Just help us!"

Before we left Barts, I managed to update George while nurses asked Carol some questions and sorted out some drugs. He looked totally stunned and said, "I'll get the car." When he pulled up to collect us, he could say very little to either of us as he helped me get Carol into the back seat.

My memory of the return journey is of tears streaming down George's cheeks as he drove us in silence. Carol slept and I tried to pray and prepare myself to share some very grim news with three kids who had already been so affected by the struggles of the Mum they adored.

On turning into our drive, Carol visibly perked up. Rarely had I seen her so glad to be home. She walked unaided to greet the kids who were waiting at the door.

George left quickly and the five family members gathered in our lounge for a conversation that none of us wanted to have but all of us needed to share. I took the phone off the hook and looked yet again, with difficulty, at the anxious, open faces of Wes, James and Mel.

Carol sat next to me on the middle sofa. I spoke first, trying to outline our conversation with Professor Lister as briefly and gently as I could. But it was Mum they were focused on and Mum they wanted to hear.

Quietly and with great vulnerability, she told them: "I can't take any more treatment. I feel that the medical profession has done all it can and they can't offer any more hope. But we can still hope. We believe in God. We can still pray and a miracle is still possible. We are not going to quit."

She was looking carefully at the kids as she spoke. She held it together until she said: "It's not me I'm worried about. It's all of you." Then she began to cry. She said: "I don't fear death. But it upsets me to think that I might not be around to see you all married and see your kids grow up."

At this we all began to lose it. Everyone moved over to put our arms round Carol. We all hugged one another and had a full-on cry together.

Then we prayed that, with all other helps gone, God would yet heal Carol and meanwhile help us be strong as a family to face all that lay ahead.

Chapter 6

....

LOOKING FOR A MIRACLE

I N THE RUN-UP TO CHRISTMAS 2001 we made a number of trips to Paget Ward at Barts. There we discovered a parallel universe of suffering and courage. Nearby was the hustle and bustle of City workers and tourists, full of life and energy. Inside Paget were thirty to forty men and women quietly fighting for life and trying to conserve what energy they had.

Some of them were just young teenagers. Others were much older. Everyone sat meekly in a large semi-circle of comfortable chairs. Some were casually reading a book or magazine; others sipped a drink or snoozed. All of them were wired up for the drip-feed of their chemotherapy treatments.

There was gentleness in the way the patients spoke to one another, so different from the strident tones on the streets outside. The nurses, native born and from overseas, brought a reassuring human touch to what could easily have become a frightening and clinical environment.

The visits for various treatments often lasted several hours and if a patient grew tired, as Carol often did, they slept on a bed at the side of the ward.

Christmas saw a brief interlude in the treatment and was spent quietly at home with family and friends. We tried to celebrate as normally as possible, each of us wanting to banish thoughts that this could be Carol's last Christmas.

Carol, with her training in home economics and skill as a cook, was well enough to direct operations, albeit with me scurrying back and forth in a new role as apprentice *sous-chef*. For the first time in my life I cooked a Christmas dinner. We had a lot of fun, often at my expense, with the kids helping me get everything organized.

I decided that cooking individual items was no big deal. Getting everything piping hot simultaneously and served effortlessly was something else altogether. It was no way as simple as Carol usually made it seem. And as for making your own gravy of an acceptable taste and texture, this was a certain recipe for *stress*.

We were not involved in any services over Christmas but the support of the church was strong. Meals lovingly prepared by friends appeared, as they did throughout Carol's illness. Catherine Lavender, a mother of two, who since her teen years had been mentored by Carol, was given star billing by the kids for her ceaseless supply of impossible-to-resist chocolate cakes.

I sent out a Christmas letter thanking so many people for their involvement in a twenty-four-hour, seven-day-a-week prayer chain. It was such a strength and comfort to know that even through the night, when Carol might wake or just be lying still with her thoughts, someone out there was remembering her in prayer.

All in all, Christmas was like being in a bubble of love and laughter, but with everyone keenly aware of the fleeting nature of bubbles.

The early days of the New Year holiday saw more trips to Barts to complete the experimental antibody treatment. We marvelled how quickly we were able to get in and out of a virtually traffic-free London.

It was a busy start to the New Year in church and I preached each Sunday. There were many gatherings in different groupings each night and most mornings, as part of a combined forty days of prayer and fasting where there was considerable concentrated prayer for Carol. Even though she had a terminal disease that was showing no sign of being arrested, a lot of people were determined to go on praying for her.

Carol was experiencing discomfort with lumps in her left breast and had lost some weight. But she was actually looking as well as she had done for some time. She was able to get out to the shops and go for short walks, weather permitting, in the neighbourhood.

We all knew that we needed an answer to prayer and we did not back off in asking and seeking for miraculous intervention. In no way did I regard this as a fool's errand. In my Master's studies in theology on the global Holy Spirit movement, which I was soon to complete, I discovered what so much of our Western cultural elite, with its closed and self-serving secular assumptions, tries to ignore: namely, that in the real world, miracles of healing do happen today. Harvard professor and author Harvey Cox noted:

> *History shows that the norm in most of the cultures of humankind… has been the complementarity of religion and healing, not their separation… the medical establishment has finally begun to recognize that there may be some genuine validity in what it had rejected for so many years as fakery and fraud.*[3]

Or, as another academic study commented:

> *For all the marvels of life in the twentieth century,*

3   Harvey Cox, *Fire from Heaven: The Rise of Pentecostal Spirituality and the Reshaping of Religion in the Twenty-First Century*, London: Cassell, 1996, pp. 108–9.

> *multitudes are unconvinced that modern theology,*
> *science or philosophy has really opened the window on*
> *the ultimate world. Scientists may try to wall out the*
> *supernatural, but the masses are scrambling around*
> *and over the walls.*[4]

Tennyson, the English poet, said simply: "More things are wrought by prayer than this world dreams of."[5]

For me the issue was not could God heal, but *would* God heal, here and now, someone I loved so much?

With this belief in the miraculous, Carol and I went to two "healing meetings" at the Kerith Centre in nearby Bracknell. The senior pastor was Ben Davies, a friend of ours. I had been to many such services and heard many first-hand accounts of recovery.

The visiting speaker was Ram Babu, an Indian evangelist and former high-caste Hindu priest, who preached to crowds of 60,000 and regularly reported many miracles in his ministry. He spoke with great authority, stressing his simple conviction that "Jesus Christ is the same, yesterday, today and forever." He spoke persuasively that miracles of healing are as possible in the West as in the East. Scores of people testified to healings in the meetings. Carol, however, was not among them.

It felt like we were at a banquet with wonderful provision on display – within arm's reach, even. Yet we were to leave empty. There had been an undeniable powerful presence in the services – a healing presence, it seemed. However, apparently it did not encompass Carol. The words of the evangelist Kathryn Kuhlman, who insisted that doctors verify the many healings at her services, came to my mind:

---

4   J. Philip Hogan quoted in Everett A. Wilson, *Strategy of the Spirit*, Carlisle: Paternoster, 1997, p. 129.
5   Alfred Lord Tennyson (1809–1892).

*You'll never know how much I hurt on the inside
when I see those who came in wheelchairs being
pushed onto the street again… but the answer I must
leave with God. No, I do not know why all are not
healed physically…* [6]

To attend a healing meeting without cynicism or scepticism, and yet not receive a cure, is, without doubt, a painful business. I felt the disappointment keenly. But Carol had been greatly boosted by her time at the services.

Ram was a compassionate and gentle man. He came over with Ben at the end of the meetings and spent some considerable time with us. He prayed for Carol and spoke many words of Scripture to her. He strongly encouraged her to focus on positive promises in Scripture and to resist fear and negative words.

For Carol this was "a big encouragement". I wrote down what she said at the time:

*Some days I have good days, some days I have bad
days, but each day I focus on God's words. When I feel
weak and I am irritated by the soreness of the tumour,
I tell myself not to focus on the circumstances but on
God's word. Like Abraham, I live with the reality of
dealing with each day, but I am living with faith that
"by his wounds we are healed" [Isaiah 53:5]. I know
there are only two possible outcomes here: life or death.
But I believe as Psalm 118:17 says: "I will not die but
live, and will proclaim what the Lord has done."*

Carol was also encouraged in her faith through another, unlikely source: a report on the *Richard and Judy* TV show, of which she

---

6   Interview in *Christianity Today*, 20 July 1973.

was a regular viewer. They featured a lady who had been told she would die of cancer. She got her church and others to pray for her. She reckoned that 10,000 people were joining in prayer. The cancer began to recede and within a month she went back for a scan, which was completely clear.

Her consultant, who was interviewed, confirmed this amazing turnaround and was prepared to accept her explanation of healing, as he had none of his own! She wrote a book on her story called *From Medicine to Miracle*.

Despite all these encouragements and the concentration of prayer at our home base and further afield, there was no escaping the fact that Carol was noticeably getting shorter of breath. By the end of January she started taking oxygen periodically to help her breathing.

On Tuesday, 5 February Professor Lister had more bad news for us. The results of a recent scan and X-ray showed that the lymphoma had spread to her lung – hence the deterioration in her breathing. It was clear that the experimental antibody treatment had not been effective.

Professor Lister wondered if Carol now wanted to immediately reconsider the option of high-dosage, high-risk chemotherapy. Her answer was the same as before. The only treatment she felt able to consent to was low-level chemotherapy treatment that could alleviate some of the symptoms and possibly extend what was, from every medical viewpoint, a limited life expectancy.

On Thursday, 7 February I wrote in a letter to our prayer supporters:

> *There is nothing really new here from what we were told in November but the reality is that time and the disease have moved on. The phrase "in God we trust"*

*is increasingly relevant and more than ever our focus
is on Him.*

*Our own family doctor visited us at home and
agreed that health was not always dependent on
medical science. He said that when many people hear
the news that we received this week they just give
up and die. As he left he told me, "Your wife is so
positive."*

Each morning and evening I sat with Carol as she lay in bed.
I did what I could to keep her positive and to feed her faith.
We were particularly struck by the persevering faith of Smith
Wigglesworth (1859–1947), a Bradford plumber who was
healed and then went round the world seeing miracles in the
biblical fashion.

Others were joining us in our prayers of faith. Church
groups and networks that we didn't even know were praying for
us in Brazil, the US and many other countries.

One friend, Mike Godward, told us how moving it was
to hear Carol's name repeatedly mentioned as hundreds of
Ugandan Christians prayed for her each week. A church in
Rouen, France, was holding a weekly prayer and fasting time for
Carol. The pastor, William Joutet, and a group of fellow leaders
got up at 3 a.m. one morning and "popped over" the Channel
just to pray with us for a short time.

A group of guys from our church – Paul Bristow, Simon
Goodison, Nigel Williams, Mark Healey, Knolly Shadrache and
Guy McDonnell – came to our home one evening and prayed
through the night with the boys and me.

By early March, despite Carol having a few tough days with
mouth ulcers which made eating painful, she was noticeably
feeling better. Her breathing was somewhat improved and she
needed oxygen less frequently.

But rapidly she became weaker as her breathing further deteriorated. Over a ten-day period she had a number of coughing spasms that were clearly difficult for her to experience. They were also distressing to observe.

Matters came to a head early on Saturday morning, 23 March. Carol awoke with severe pain. She was never one to complain or dramatize. In fact, she was the polar opposite of a hypochondriac. But now she struggled between breaths to say, "I need help quickly."

The kids sat with her while I packed a bag. The emergency services seemed to take an age to arrive but actually they made it to our home very quickly. She was taken by ambulance first to Wexham Park Hospital in Slough and then on to Barts. I sat with her as she lay weakly in the ambulance. We said little, as she was trying to conserve her limited energy.

I wanted to be strong for her but inside I felt very apprehensive. Then I looked out of the ambulance and saw a sight that cheered me. We passed a double-decker bus, picking up a large group of children for our Kidz Klub. Both Carol and I had long wanted to see this ministry established and now hundreds of kids were coming along every week. I told her what I had just seen and we both smiled for the first time that morning.

On arrival at the now-familiar Barts, Carol was very poorly. She looked so grey and drawn. She appeared to have aged years over the past few weeks. The hair that had grown back after her initial recovery was now gone again. She seemed such a small figure in a large bed. Talking was an effort for her. So mostly we just sat quietly beside her as she rested. The boys looked anxious as they saw their Mum go in and out of a troubled sleep. But by the evening Carol was in a noticeably better condition. The doctors suspected that she had picked up an infection but were confident that it could soon be brought under control.

We left the hospital more hopeful, even though we were all drained after a long rollercoaster day of emotions. Melody herself was unwell with tonsillitis and was being looked after by friends. I felt for her, that she could not be with either her Mum or her Dad at this time. James stayed up in London with me, while Wes went back to cover home base.

Over the next few days, in addition to the superb medical attention, Carol was ministered to by one of Africa's foremost Christian leaders, Dr Enoch Adeboye, the head of the huge, global, Nigerian-based Redeemed Christian Church of God.[7] Invited by our friends Agu and Ify Irukwu, pastors of Jesus House in London, Dr Adeboye took time out to come with his wife to pray for Carol. This statesmanlike man with a strong aura of spiritual authority spoke to Carol with great compassion. She visibly brightened during the visit and there was a tangible presence of peace in her hospital room. Our faith was strengthened. Was this to be the point of breakthrough?

How we were factoring everything at the time was evident in an update to our prayer supporters:

> *Despite everything I see and know all too clearly (even though I am no escapist and though I don't know how), I believe the miracle of Carol's healing will take place and she will recover. Nothing is too hard for the Lord. Nothing is impossible with God.*

These last words were soon to seem very appropriate. For just a few days after Carol had been so suddenly admitted to hospital, we experienced something that certainly appeared impossible at the time. Her condition stabilized to the point that she was allowed home on Tuesday, 26 March.

---

7   *Newsweek* magazine named Dr Adeboye as one of the fifty most powerful people in the world, December 2008.

On top of that good news, three days after her discharge from hospital, Carol was well enough for us to have a totally unexpected five-day Easter break with the family, just a few miles along the south coast from where we had our honeymoon.

Just one week on from our dramatic rush to Barts, Carol was sitting comfortably on the beach in Poole, Dorset, enjoying some unseasonably warm weather. She looked as well as we had seen her for many weeks. Was this all down to medical attention or was something else going on? Could it be that a miracle was in progress?

As the five of us set out on Good Friday, 29 March, I felt both hope and relief. After all the intensity of the days at Barts when Carol was so ill, it was joy beyond words to have her out and about with all the family packed and heading off for a break. It felt so much like old times, normal times.

I think we all felt like we had suddenly been released from prison. Perhaps we had been, despite the oxygen canisters in the car that indicated that we were only on a temporary mercy visit to the outside world.

Each of us focused on making the most of the precious time together. What mattered was that we could be alone with the people we loved the most. Nothing else was important at that moment. Even the inevitable bank holiday traffic jam seemed totally inconsequential.

Our days were spent lazily, eating in at a home that friends had kindly lent us, watching movies, playing a few games, reading and chatting. We had family prayers for Carol's healing and we gave thanks that we could be together. But mostly we relaxed and enjoyed the gift of shared time that we were so suddenly enjoying.

The sea air seemed to be a tonic to Carol. She was able to walk short distances. For the first time in weeks she did not need any oxygen. We all enjoyed just being out and about with her and with one another.

I was touched by how the kids took each opportunity to cuddle up to Carol. I too held her often, though to hold her was to know how fragile she was. We all told each other frequently how much we loved each other, but then we always had done so.

In so many ways it was such a happy time. But, for all the sudden improvement, the sentence of death had not been lifted. It was to be the last time we ever had a holiday together.

Chapter 7

LAST DAYS

A S AN UNSEASONABLY WARM spring turned into a sunny summer, the shadows were rapidly lengthening for Carol. Events were now to move quickly, although at the time, a day, and more particularly a night, felt like someone had pressed a slow-motion button.

For the first two weeks in April after the Poole trip, Carol continued to do relatively well. She was able to sit out in the garden and go on short walks. But by 19 April she had picked up an infection. So once more we helped her into the car and took her on the familiar drive through central London.

She stayed overnight at Barts for observation. We were relieved that she was able to come home the next day, having been put on a course of antibiotics.

There was, however, no disguising that she was showing signs of a new phase of deterioration. She was increasingly weak and breathless and needed oxygen periodically. Less than a week since her last visit, she needed to go back to the hospital. This time she stayed a few days longer.

Carol was put on a further course of antibiotics for an infection and received some treatment aimed at alleviating her current breathlessness. By 28 April she had improved enough to come home. After five nights in her own bed, she spent the sixth back at Barts for further observation and treatment.

This yo-yoing up and down to hospital then continued with a further six nights at home. All this was physically and emotionally draining to Carol and, in truth, to all of us.

Everyone rallied together – friends, doctors, carers and family – to make things comfortable for Carol at home, where she was the most happy. My stalwart friend Terry would regularly disappear with empty oxygen canisters and reappear hauling heavy new ones. Other friends would man the phones and bring in food.

Wes, having put travel and career plans on hold, did various household chores and helped me with whatever cropped up. He also daily went out on walks to pray. I saw the same determination to do what he could to "fight" for his Mum as I had witnessed in his commitment to win gold in his rowing career.

James and Mel would chat with their Mum for as long as they could before she insisted that they find a quiet space to prepare for their imminent exams. It was a hard call when exams could always be left and taken later. James was about to take his final exams for his degree, and Mel needed to achieve high A level results for university. But I saw the wisdom, as well as the selflessness, in Carol's approach. She did not want them constantly focused on her sickness and thought that they should do their best to get on with life even when things were tough.

And with such uncertainty about the future, the kids also had the benefit of completing their current level of studies with Carol around to encourage them. I imagine that the scenario of them suspending their studies and then later having to continue them if she was not around was also in her thoughts, though we never discussed this.

But how long would Carol be around? All of us could see that she was finding each day a greater struggle. For all her bravery and positive outlook, she clearly could not carry on for long like this. She was increasingly breathless and on oxygen most of the time.

Something had to give soon. And it did. By Friday, 10 May Carol was too ill to be helped at home. She was readmitted to Barts for what was to become a critical week-long stay.

By now she was very weak and in need of regular blood transfusions. It was often an effort for her to speak. She was now unable to walk even short distances to the bathroom. Her weight had dropped alarmingly. I was determined to stay close to her.

The nursing staff of Bodley Scott 2 were very sympathetic and found me a temporary bed in a little room nearby. I was able to be on call for Carol 24/7 to help her in every practical way that I could.

I would see her and kiss her last thing at night and very early in the morning. I would always say a little prayer with her and give her a word of Scripture. Even though her body was decaying, we both knew how much this fed her spirit.

She would just hold my hand or thank me so gratefully. I just felt powerless to do anything that would stop the merciless advance of rogue cells in her frail body. So mostly I simply sat near her, ready to give the occasional sip of water. I marvelled at Carol's resilience of spirit as she faced each day with increasing weariness.

Late one night, with the hospital lights low, she pulled me close and whispered in my ear, "I've been listening to a track from *The Prince of Egypt*. There's a line that says, 'Though hope is frail, it's hard to kill.'"

In the darkness I welled up. I did so again later as I listened with new ears to the stirring music and lyrics that vocalized Carol's feelings so well:

There can be miracles when you believe
Though hope is frail, it's hard to kill;
Who knows what miracles you can achieve
When you believe, somehow you will
You will when you believe

They don't always happen when you ask
And it's easy to give in to your fear
But when you're blinded by your pain
Can't see the way clear through the rain
A small but still resilient voice
Says hope is very near.[8]

Carol, for sure, was not giving in to fear and, in sharing this with me, I knew she wanted to strengthen my faith too.

Thankfully, she was not "blinded" by pain but she was increasingly experiencing discomfort. It became a challenge even to arrange pillows in such a way that she felt able to rest easily.

A special high-tech adjustable bed was found for her. I remember her sighing with relief when she settled on it. Her gratitude was humbling.

The kids took it in turns to come up. I well remember one surprise visit from Mel who was supposed to be studying. When she walked in, Carol's face was instantly transformed into a picture of childlike wonder and delight.

Mel carefully found a spot to sit on her Mum's bed. Carol gently stroked her as she eagerly listened to the latest news from home and school. This unexpected girls' time resulted in me being summarily and good-naturedly dismissed to the nearby Carluccio's, where Carol liked me to buy her some quality coffee.

---

8   Stephen Schwartz, "When you believe" (Dream Works animated feature *The Prince of Egypt*, 1998).

This stands out in my memory, as it seemed such a moment of relief, albeit brief, from the ever-present inner tension of watching a terminally sick loved one slowly slip from you. Sometimes, when Carol was sleeping, I just had to get out and go for a walk. Irrationally, I felt guilty that I was able to leave the hospital whenever I felt like it.

Stepping into the frenetic pace of London life, with all its movement and focus, contrasted sharply with the oppressive awareness that Carol was now so immobile and that our world as a family was increasingly out of focus.

I found it a comfort to be able to pop into St Paul's Cathedral, just a few minutes' walk away. Amid the tourists, there were clearly others like me who had just come to pray. I looked up to the vast dome and asked again for a great miracle. "Please, Lord. Just do it. I do believe, but help my unbelief."

On my walks near the hospital I looked around for any sign that would give me courage or hope. St Paul's itself, the iconic image of survival during the Blitz in World War II, showed that it was possible to make it through the fiercest onslaughts. An unexpected inscription on the London Wall seemed to jump out at me with these bold words: "In God is all our trust."

The front of Barts itself carried an inspirational memorial to the courage of the Scottish "Braveheart", William Wallace, who "fought dauntlessly in the face of fearful odds and great hardship". Not unlike Carol, I thought. What a fight she had put up! And she was still fighting.

By 16 May, after a week that had been almost unrelentingly bleak, Carol was visibly brighter. Once more she had rallied to the point where she was well enough to come home. In my view she, more than President Bill Clinton, deserved to be called "the Comeback Kid".

For two weeks from the middle of May, Carol was able to

rest at home. She was feeling more on an even keel. We were able to establish a routine of some normality. Every day, morning and evening, I read passages from the Bible on faith, hope and perseverance. And every day we prayed for grace for the day and for healing for Carol's tumour-riddled body.

I passed on stories of people who had conquered adversity, and shared encouraging letters from friends. Carol did not want to hear negative talk or hear from people who would communicate negativity. She wanted strength, not sympathy. She told me repeatedly: "I'm going to fight this. We're not giving in!"

Each morning, after our time together, Wes and James would take it in turns to pick up their increasingly light mother from our upstairs bedroom and gently carry her down to the lounge. The other brother would carry the oxygen tank. Every day Carol insisted on dressing, keeping a smart appearance and sitting in a chair downstairs.

Every evening the boys would take their Mum and the ubiquitous oxygen tank back upstairs. Carol joked with them about how many girls would love to be carried by these toned athletes. They did their best to smile.

In the afternoon Carol would walk across the lounge to a special bed which had been brought in and have a nap. But she was set against spending any more time in bed than she needed.

Mostly we limited visits to longstanding friends. But one day James came in with a new friend from church who was also a golfing buddy. He was a dark-haired and personable nineteen-year-old South African, a combination that did not escape Carol's attention. When he left she told me what an impressive guy the young Johannes Erasmus was, adding with a raised eyebrow and a wink towards Mel that he was "a bit of all right!"

Though Carol was not to know it, she was, in fact, having her first and only meeting with her future son-in-law. Melody would later marry knowing that her mother had approved of her husband and that her husband had in turn been inspired by the positive attitude of her Mum.

The low-key daily home routine was only interrupted on 31 May when Carol was back in hospital overnight for some palliative treatment. She was readmitted for a further (and, as events were to transpire, final) overnight stay in Barts on 7 June.

The next three weeks were very peaceful, as outside visits were limited and calls diverted. There was a serenity and quiet in Carol and in the home. The sun shone in on her and I can picture her now with her long legs casually stretched out on a footrest. As often as not, our eccentric white-and-ginger cat, Wally, who followed me dog-like on my neighbourhood walks, was to be found purring on her lap.

She sat peacefully by a French window that opened out to our garden and a patio that I had filled with a variety of tubs of colourful flowers. I displayed them with a flourish but I had little idea what they were and had relied heavily on the advice of the local garden centre.

This was a source of some amusement to Carol, who had always shown far more interest in the garden than I had. She had long since given up on her habit in the early days of our marriage of telling me to "go and subdue the earth" rather than watch rugby.

Our laughter, talks and prayers in these days were some of the tenderest moments of our marriage. One evening in mid June around the time of my 52nd birthday, we had a heart to heart about our faith and the future.

We had been friends for thirty-four years, and married for nearly twenty-nine, but I was also her pastor. I did not want to fail her in this role on account of the closeness of our relationship.

So I asked her: "Carol, if there is to be no miracle of healing, are you really ready to die?"

She looked at me quizzically as if this were a trick question. "Yes, I am ready," she said.

I pressed her further, perhaps more for my sake than hers. "Carol, I know we have always believed and preached all this, but if this is really it, do you know for sure that your sins are forgiven and that you will be with Jesus in heaven?"

Carol looked straight at me and gave the kind of smile a kindly teacher might give a struggling student. "Of course I know I am going to heaven," she said decisively.

Then she added: "I am ready, if this is the time. But I'm not sure it is. So we should keep on praying and believing for a miracle."

"Agreed," I said. "We will pray on."

Carol was also determined that we should not only pray on but also get on with making the most of every day. She insisted that I attend my nephew Gareth's wedding on 22 June. I was pleased to see a young couple so happy, but my heart and thoughts were with my own bride of long ago, who was now in sickness, not in health.

While I was at the wedding Carol thought about her own sons' future weddings. She told Terry Beasley's wife Margaret, who was looking after her, "I know the boys' wives are out there and I know they will meet them soon."

The next week was not so easy for Carol but she was still well enough to see a few friends. It seemed almost like the good old days when Simon and Louise Goodison, whom Carol and I had long mentored and been on holiday with, came round for the Thursday evening. It was a relaxed and uplifting time with easy talk and laughter.

I recall looking across the room at Carol. She was wearing grey slacks, a purple top and a trendy bandana. She looked so composed, and to me, beautiful. I remember thinking that someone who looked so cool couldn't possibly be so ill. I couldn't begin to imagine that, less than forty-eight hours later, she would no longer be with us.

The next day was a big day in several ways. Mel was taking her last exam and I was half-heartedly making arrangements for my Master's graduation for the following day. Carol insisted I go, so we planned for Margaret to look after her again.

I drove Mel to and from Reading for her exam and shared her relief that it was all over. Carol was delighted for her girl. She had done it, despite everything. Early that evening we had a muted family celebration.

Carol wanted an early night but she told Mel to go through with attending an end-of-term ball. Carol was keen for her to wear an expensive purple gown that she had bought for her many months before. Mel, with her blonde hair swept up, looked stunning. Carol's delight was complete as she saw the youngest of her kids go out and on her way.

I should have known that Carol was hanging on for this. I doubt if she consciously gave up at that point. But that night, in the early hours, her resistance to overwhelming odds dramatically and distressingly collapsed. The doctors came quickly but they could not, for some hours, bring her suffering to an acceptable level of control.

By morning more help kept arriving from nurses, doctors and friends. Carol was able to talk with us but she did not have strength for much conversation. She responded with a smile or squeeze of the hand as we took our fading opportunities to say again that we loved her. But she was very weak. For the first time, she was in no state to insist on coming downstairs.

By lunchtime, graduation plans now cancelled, she was sleeping heavily. The kids and I took it in turns to sit with her. There was no more anyone could do. But, mercifully, Carol was comfortable.

Just after 2 p.m. I noticed that the colour was changing on Carol's face. Her breathing was becoming laboured. I quickly called the kids in.

I quietly told them: "Your Mum is about to go." James came up to me and slipped something in my hand. I looked down. It was his Henley medal. I nodded. I knew what he was saying. They had won their race right at the last. Now here we were, with the finish line in sight for Carol, but still in faith for a miracle result.

If ever there was a time for divine intervention, this was it. But there was to be no last-minute reprieve. There was to be no earthly victor's rostrum for Carol. Her time had come.

The kids and I sat around on the bed with Carol. She was propped up, peacefully resting on pillows. We held hands with her and one another. If Carol could still hear, I wanted her to hear what we would say now.

I told her how much we all loved her. I said a short prayer, thanking God for her and for her love to her family. Then I committed her to the loving care of her Heavenly Father.

As I recited the psalmist's words, "I will dwell in the house of the Lord forever", Carol gave two deep sighs.

And then she was gone, at 2.24 p.m. on Saturday, 29 June 2002, with the sun shining in on her.

Chapter 8

WILL OUR ANCHOR HOLD?

W E STAYED BY CAROL'S LIFELESS body for some time. She looked so peaceful. All traces of pain in her appearance had suddenly disappeared. The transformation was remarkable.

We kept focusing on Carol as if mesmerized. There she was, still propped up on pillows in our bed as she had been so many times. But she was just not with us any more. She had gone into eternity in a moment.

I studied the faces of the kids who had just seen death up close and personal for the first time. There were no tears, just heavy expressions of stunned disbelief.

None of us said a word. Then for a while we held hands as a family of five for one last time. Wes prayed a prayer that was painful in its intensity. I prayed too, thanking God for every memory of Carol and asking that He would give us courage in the days ahead to face our challenges as Carol had faced hers.

Some more minutes passed slowly until I managed to ask quietly, "Are we ready to let her go now?" The kids nodded their agreement. Then they took it in turns to stroke Carol's face or hands. One by one they gave her a kiss and said their goodbyes.

Mel was the first to leave the room. I went after her and

found her sitting alone on a chair in the middle of the garden. She was holding her head in her hands. She looked utterly bereft. She wanted to be left alone.

I went back upstairs to find Wes in tears. I held him tight and cried with him. James looked in a daze. I hugged him close too. I asked them if they would wait while I had some moments alone in the room with Carol.

I don't know how long I was there but I cried and sighed a lot. I looked at her thin and ravaged body and felt a sense of relief that my lovely darling wife was no longer in pain. But, oh God! How empty it already seemed without her.

As memories flooded back, I reflected on our marriage and on vows that had now reached their fulfilment... for better, for worse... in sickness and in health... till death us do part.

I asked the boys to join me as I took off the wedding ring that I had given Carol nearly twenty-nine years before and the twenty-fifth anniversary ring that I had bought for our second honeymoon. And then from either side of me they locked their arms around me and held me in a great grip.

The next hours were a blur of conversations, tearful phone calls and the arrival of friends who stood with us as Carol's body was so functionally zipped up in a bag and carried from our home by the undertakers.

Our house underwent a rapid makeover as the temporary bed in the lounge was removed along with the oxygen tanks, the packs of tablets and the varied assortment of items necessarily connected with the care of the terminally ill. Abruptly it all vanished – just like Carol.

Late that evening, I gathered the kids and some close friends together for a time of prayer. I said I wanted us to thank God for Carol's life and to make a choice that we would still worship God in our time of acute pain.

Carol Richards.

Pastor Wes Richards.

Wesley and James enjoying their success at sculling.

The family with James after his crew won at Henley Royal Regatta, July 1997.

Carol and Mel relaxing in St Louis.

Carol's gravestone, imported from South Africa.

IN
TREASURED
MEMORY OF
CAROL ANN RICHARDS
MUCH LOVED WIFE, MOTHER, FRIEND
AND PARTNER IN THE GOSPEL
BORN DECEMBER 3RD 1950
GRADUATED TO HEAVEN JUNE 29TH 2002
THE LORD WATCHES OVER YOU
PSALM 121:5

The Richards family on their trip to America after Carol died.

Forging links in Colombia – with Colombian President Álvaro Uribe Velez in January 2008.

Wes with Pastors César and Claudia Castellanos, good friends from Colombia.

Wes speaking at a big outdoor event at Simon Bolivar park – Bogotá, Colombia.

Developing relationships in South Africa – Wes preaching to the kids and parents at a rugby ground in Robertson.

Wes at the Cape of Good Hope, South Africa.

Celebrating the third wedding in front of the Twelve Apostles, Cape Town.

Wes and Gert with their sons and grandsons.

Wes and Carol.

Wesley and Wilana.

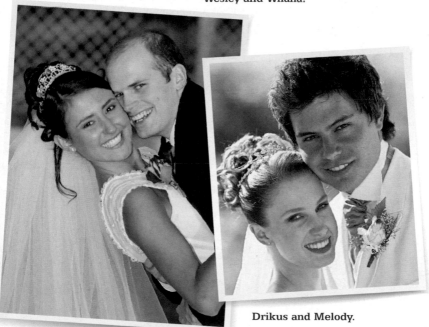

James and Vasti.

Drikus and Melody.

Picture proof of how much the family has grown! This was taken outside Holy Trinity Garrison Church, Windsor, in September 2011 when babies Eliana (held by Vasti) and Caleb (held by Melody) were dedicated.

The whole family being anointed as pastors, along with faithful friends Terry and Margaret, November 2009.

Everyone agreed to this and we joined hands together. The act of praying caused my own tears to flow and I could hear the soft weeping of others. But there was also a real sense of peace that settled over us as I quietly repeated the words of Job 1:21 (NKJV): "The Lord gave and the Lord has taken away; blessed be the name of the Lord."

That first night without Carol, however, seemed to last for ever. Sleep just would not come. My mind was in overdrive replaying the events of her passing and trying to think of all the planning that was needed for the funeral.

Over the next few days Terry Beasley, with his background as a former senior welfare officer with the British Post Office, was a star helping us deal with such mundane matters as registering the death and liaising with doctors and undertakers – all details that can cause the newly bereaved so much anxiety.

Our home was like a London train station at rush hour as friends popped in and church leaders came to agree on the order of service. I wanted to do my personal and professional best to honour Carol and also to make sure that all the hospitality, transportation and accommodation were well organized for all the friends who would be coming from near and far. In truth, our leadership team was capable of handling things without me, but I just wanted to do something, anything, which would represent some kind of order and purpose in my life at a moment of fundamental disorientation.

I also wanted to be strong for the kids and to give them a lift by delivering what I hoped would be a fitting eulogy to their beloved Mum. The kids had similar ideas and were insistent that they each wanted to speak too. I was not altogether sure about this, as I thought it would be more of an emotional ordeal than they anticipated. In the event, they were a great strength to me and a memorable inspiration to the congregation of around 600 people who gathered at the Parish Church of St John the Baptist next to Windsor Castle.

The weather on the day of the funeral, 8 July 2002, was a reflection of what I was feeling as we were driven to the church. It was mostly grey and overcast with the occasional burst of sunshine. There was warmth as we talked with family and friends. But I was aware of a hovering feeling of oppressiveness as we arrived for Carol's funeral in the heart of Windsor where we had so often enjoyed carefree walks.

I sighed involuntarily as Carol's coffin was lifted out of the funeral car and onto the shoulders of some of the leaders of the church. I tried with only partial success to switch off my emotions. I noticed that the boys in particular had grim expressions on their faces as we followed the coffin up the old stone steps of the church. Mel was composed but subdued and stayed close to me.

Once inside, however, we were buoyed by the sight of so many people gathered with us in our time of grief. It had been comforting to know that so many people were planning to attend, but the actual reality of seeing them all there, plus others we had not expected, almost cut through my defences.

There were so many young people – school friends, church friends and university friends – many of whom had sat around our table at home. There were rowing friends, coaches, parents, sons and daughters and teachers and governors from The Windsor Boys' School. There were community figures, neighbours, many church members and Christian leaders from other church circles in the UK and overseas.

Mike and Linda Peters and their daughter Erin, for whom Carol and I were her "British parents", had come over from the States. William Joutet was there from France. Kathryn Porter, whose Christian work in Russia we had long supported, battled red tape and got a last-minute flight. Philippe Ouedraogo, head of an outstanding Christian relief ministry in Burkina Faso that we had long partnered with, was there along with other friends from Spain, Germany, Argentina and Nigeria.

Carol would have been amazed by the turnout, I thought. What would probably have pleased her more was that so many great people were giving her family such support.

Yet for all the goodwill flowing towards us, there was a subdued, if not apprehensive atmosphere as the service began. That atmosphere was soon to change in a remarkable way that few present would ever forget, and certainly not the four of us.

Something went on in that service that brought great reserves of strength and faith to us at one of the lowest moments in our lives. It started with the singing of a great old hymn that I had chosen and which I had known since I was a kid. Its title was a question: "Will your anchor hold?"[9]

As we started to move down the aisle of the expansive Victorian church, Simon Goodison, who had visited us just before Carol died, powerfully sang, unaccompanied, the penetrating first words of the old hymn:

> *Will your anchor hold in the storms of life,*
> *When the clouds unfold their wings of strife;*
> *When the strong tides lift and the cables strain,*
> *Will your anchor drift or firm remain?*

As the coffin was placed near the pulpit, a wave of sound broke around us and from the galleries above us, as the musicians, singers and congregation joined Simon in a chorus of response to this very pertinent question:

---

9   Priscilla Jane Owens (1829–1899), "We have an anchor". Music by William J. Kirkpatrick.

We have an anchor that keeps the soul
Steadfast and sure while the billows roll
Fastened to the Rock which cannot move
Grounded firm and deep in the Saviour's love.

As we stood there in the front pew I was increasingly heartened by the fervour of the congregational singing and the truths that they were declaring. Even in the eye of our storm we had a secure anchor.

It is safely moored, 'twill the storm withstand
For 'tis well secured by the Saviour's hand;
And the cables passed from His heart to mine
Can defy the blast through strength divine.

It will firmly hold in the floods of death
When the waters cold chill our latest breath
On the rising tide it can never fail
While our hopes abide within the veil.[10]

As the congregation sang each verse with mounting conviction and volume, there was a corresponding and noticeable build-up of hope. Each time they repeated the chorus it was with increased strength. And each time I felt my spirits lift.

The last verse was sung with an assurance of overcoming faith that could only happen, I thought, with a congregation containing so many Christian believers:

When our eyes behold through the gathering night
The city of gold, our harbour bright
We shall anchor fast by the heavenly shore
With the storms all past for evermore.

---

10   This is a biblical reference from Hebrews 6:19–20 referring to close fellowship with God.

By the time this first hymn ended my perspective had shifted from what was happening with us on earth to the hope of heaven, of which Carol herself had been so calmly confident in her last days. I looked at the kids and saw that they were more peaceful and relaxed after what we all had just experienced.

I was glad that was the case, for the three of them were about to pay their individual tributes to Carol. I gave Mel a squeeze of the hand as she left my side and walked past her Mum's coffin to speak first.

The congregation became very quiet at the sight of this diminutive eighteen-year-old readying herself to speak. When she did, it was with great clarity, reality and even humour. She wanted to tell them all "just how special my Mum was":

> *My Mum was and is simply the best. Words cannot really say how much I love, appreciate and value her as a mother. It is painful to lose a mother but also I have lost my best friend.*
>
> *There are so many happy and fun memories that at times it almost seems difficult to be sad. She was always full of common sense, which I think she has definitely passed on to me and maybe my brothers too.*
>
> *More than anything my Mum has taught me to have strength – strength to continue fighting when all seems hopeless. Her determination and faith is something I will aspire to. She fought so hard these past eighteen months but remained calm and full of life. She never wanted us to fuss over her. She is my inspiration and I told her so the day she died.*
>
> *I will enjoy life because of her. Mum taught us how to make the most out of life. She has taught*

*me and us as a family to laugh and have fun when
we are sad and to have faith and hope despite
unanswered questions.*

As Mel walked calmly to her seat I felt a great paternal affection for her. I noticed that people were wiping away tears. One of them, the Reverend Nicky Gumbel, the leader of the international Alpha course, later summed up the experience of many when he said: "I cried through the whole service."

James was next up with a tribute that I found very poignant. Standing tall and slim, he looked the part of a young international sportsman. He was quick to acknowledge his Mum's influence on his life:

*I thank God for giving me such a beautiful and loving
Mum. I remember sitting by her bedside looking
into her eyes. I could see how much she loved and
understood me and I could see the peace and strength
that she had.*

*She supported me every step along the way. Mum
modelled the very best attributes – love, joy, peace,
patience, kindness, goodness, faithfulness, gentleness
and self-control. She had great dignity and an inner
strength based on a personal relationship with Jesus
Christ.*

*Even through her illness she refused to be ruled
by the probable. She lived her life believing in the
possible.*

*She was not only a great friend and mother. She
was a great wife and balanced person. Mum and Dad
have set me an example of love, fun and commitment
that I will strive to honour and follow all the days of
my life.*

> *We were her ambition in life. And she has set*
> *us up for life. She invested so much time, care and*
> *interest. I am grateful beyond words for everything she*
> *ever did for me. She loved me and she believed in me.*
> *I will never forget that.*

I felt for Wes, who had listened to his brother's vulnerable oration and now had to deliver his own. But he too stood tall, with equal dignity and poise. He spoke movingly of "a wonderful Mum, wife and person".

> *Words cannot convey my feelings for her. I thank*
> *God for every year and moment with her. She loved*
> *me unconditionally, supported me continually and*
> *gave me a great sense of self-belief. She helped me and*
> *trained me during those younger, formative years,*
> *letting me loose when the time had come.*
>
> *From then on she became my greatest supporter.*
> *Thanks to her, a chubby baby turned himself into a*
> *lightweight rower. A homework-fearing kid became a*
> *Master's graduate. I take great pride in knowing that*
> *I made her proud.*
>
> *With her encouragement, fears and doubts were*
> *turned to victory and triumph. Due to this coaching,*
> *obstacles are now challenges to be overcome as I*
> *continue onward in life.*
>
> *It has been a long and hard journey in recent*
> *days. We had our laughs at her bedside and we shed*
> *our tears. I want to take the pain away from James*
> *and Mel and save Dad from further grief, but I know*
> *I cannot. To feel such a deep and hurting pain is only*
> *possible if you have loved with an equal intensity.*

As Wes left the lectern and gave me a nod of encouragement, I could see that the three tributes by the children had moved many. They were a much harder act to follow than I had imagined. I took a moment to compose myself as I faced the congregation.

I too spoke of Carol as "a lady of great love. She loved her children, she loved me, she loved people, she loved life and she loved God."

I recounted how we had fallen in love as teenagers.

> And the unfashionable truth really is that in the thirty-four years since, twenty-nine of them as a married couple, our love grew stronger and stronger, never more so than in these last testing months.
>
> Carol had a great gift of making people feel special. James has often announced to the family, "I'm her favourite!" And everyone has always smiled securely because we all knew that actually, we were!
>
> Carol was proud to be a wife and mother. She didn't want to be liberated from these roles. She wanted to be liberated to them.
>
> It was in her home life that she found her greatest security, fulfilment and fun and made her greatest impact.
>
> Our home was open to so many friends, including so many students. Children and young people loved to be with Carol and she loved to be with them. For she was a young spirit and a free spirit.
>
> Carol was a great judge of people and could spot both reality and pretence with unerring accuracy. To be sure, she had little time for phoniness and empty religion. But time and again Carol somehow managed to be incredibly non-judgmental about people.

> *Carol's faith was grounded in the unconditional grace and mercy of God. All through the years, through many pleasures and pressures alike, her faith in Jesus Christ has been simple, profound and unwavering. She knew that you didn't have to understand God to follow Him. You have to trust Him.*
>
> *Like many of us, I would have liked Carol here much longer. But I am so grateful to have had Carol for so long. I am so glad that we took our marriage vows. And I am so glad we kept them. I am honoured to have been her husband and I am honoured to have served her. Carol was simply lovely in every way. Her fragrance will linger on always.*

As I walked back to the front pew I felt relieved that we had all been able to communicate our tributes. At the same time I was almost expecting that Carol would be waiting for me as I retook my seat. This time, however, there was not a reassuringly familiar whisper in my ear, "You did well, Wes", nor even one of her smiles that said, "You'll do better next time!"

The congregation, which contained many non-churchgoers, continued to listen attentively as various gifted leaders from near and far took part. But it was the family emphasis that stood out most strongly and the references to Carol's deep and down-to-earth faith. Mike Peters captured this well as he recounted our moose-hunting escapades and recalled many conversations by log fires or while picnicking in the great American outdoors:

> *Carol was a pragmatically spiritual person. Wes and I would come up with wonderful ideas… we thought – but if it didn't pass the Carol test it wouldn't work.*

She would say, "Oh, nobody cares about that!" Well,
she just threw out hours of discussion.

This very accurate insight made me laugh along with many others who knew Carol well.

Pete added, "Carol wasn't just a Mum to fellow believers; she was a Mum to anyone that came into her house. To see the power of the living faith that is demonstrated in a loving family makes much more impact than any sermon ever could. Carol demonstrated that kind of faith."

In closing Pete recounted how he had recently graduated "with what men call the highest degree, but it was not. The highest degree is the degree that Carol has earned by passing the greatest test. She has graduated into heaven's glory."

As a token of his honour for Carol, he placed on her coffin the tassel from his PhD graduation mortar-board and declared: "Carol Ann Richards, *semper fidelis*, always faithful."

I was touched by my friend's gesture, knowing how many years he had worked to earn that tassel.

The emotional moments continued as the combined funeral and memorial service concluded with the powerful singing of some appropriate worship songs and two of Carol's favourite hymns: Keith Green's "There is a Redeemer" and the Welsh classic, "Here is love vast as the ocean".

Then church leaders and members, women and men and younger and older, formed a guard of honour as the coffin was carried out of the church to the strains of Carol and Mel's favourite Westlife song, "Flying Without Wings".

As we left the church I was grateful that I felt far more uplifted than when we entered it. I was pleased to see that the kids were on an even keel. But I was already emotionally trying to prepare myself for what I knew (from long experience of conducting funerals) was usually the hardest part of the day: the burial service in the graveyard.

Wes, James, Mel and I formed a huddle for some moments of prayer together as around 300 people joined us in a large circle for the short open-air service. There was no music but the outdoor congregation became an impressive choir as, with rain lightly falling on us, they sang "Amazing Grace". For sure, John Newton's experience was also Carol's:

Through many dangers, toils and snares
I have already come
'Tis grace that brought me safe thus far
And grace will lead me home.[11]

With these convictions of God's overriding providence and mercy once more impressed on us, the coffin carrying Carol's mortal remains was laid in the earth under a towering English oak tree. The kids and I took it in turns to throw in some soil. I paused for a while and stared into the ground. Carol's words at the start of her ordeal came to mind: "I never thought that it would come to this." But then some words of Jesus came to me, pushing out all other thoughts:

I am the resurrection and the life. He who believes in
me will live, even though he dies; and whoever lives
and believes in me will never die… Because I live you
will also live.

John 11:25–26

Like the drizzle that was now falling more heavily, I felt a descending and increasing peace that I would meet Carol again.

---

11   John Newton (1725-1807), "Amazing Grace" (1779).

Or as my Dad had said in his last words to me, "I will see you in the morning."

With those thoughts foremost in my mind, I hugged family and friends and left the graveside, little realizing that it would soon contain an unexpected sign of a link between our past and our future.

Once the ground had settled there would be a headstone bearing these simple words:

> *In treasured memory of Carol Ann Richards, much loved wife, mother, friend and partner in the gospel. Born December 3, 1950. Graduated to Heaven June 29, 2002. The Lord watches over you, Psalm 121:5.*

The blue-grey marble headstone that I was to choose, although I did not realize its place of origin at the time, was imported from South Africa.

Chapter 9

NOW WHAT?

OUR HOUSE SEEMED peculiarly empty the morning after the funeral. Everything was clean and back in place but the sparkle in the home was missing. I felt it acutely. So did the kids.

There was no disguising our shared sense of bewilderment. One by one we had wandered into the kitchen, the epicentre of Carol's domain. We looked at each other as if to say, "Now what?"

After eighteen months of intense activity with hospital trips, treatments, home care and, finally, all the arrangements and emotions of the funeral, everything had come to a very sharp stop. Suddenly we didn't have to rush around. We didn't have to be anywhere. We didn't have to be on a state of high alert day and night. We could do whatever we wanted. We could now get on with our lives. We were free. Only it didn't seem like that, for sure.

How exactly were we going to simply "move on", without such a mainstay of our family's life? And anyway, even if we figured out how we could, I was not sure that we wanted to move on at this moment. In fact, I was sure that we did not. We had said our farewells to Carol at the cemetery but that didn't mean we wanted to let go.

We wanted to do everything to keep Carol "alive" and part

of our family. So we talked about her at every opportunity. We read and re-read what everyone had said about her in a book of remembrance. We got out all the family photograph albums and reminisced about her.

I looked at a particularly gorgeous picture of Carol – beautiful, stylish and smiling so naturally. I wished for her to somehow walk out of the frame and into my arms.

I tried to will myself to hear her laugh. I wanted to remember her touch. I held her clothes against my face.

The clothes affected me more than I had bargained for. The drawers were packed with clothes for all seasons. The wardrobe was full of dresses, skirts and gowns that Carol would never wear again. Just to look at certain outfits would remind me of her taste, elegance and zest for life. I could still smell the fragrance of her favourite perfumes.

What was I to do with them now? Just put them in a plastic bag and give them away? That didn't seem right. This was Carol's stuff. Even so, I didn't feel I could look at them every time I went to a bedroom that was now no longer ours, but mine. I knew at some point I must get rid of them or risk living in a museum. But in these raw, early days Mel particularly didn't want to even talk of moving them and I was comfortable in delaying a decision for the moment.

I feared – I think we all feared – that somehow we might forget Carol. As if we ever could. So for now we tried to make time stand still, as the rest of world kept revolving as usual.

Of course, our bereavement, when set against global tragedies like wars, poverty and disease, seemed insignificant in the big scheme of things. But if the poet John Donne was right in saying that "any man's death diminishes me because I am involved in Mankind", then I wondered how much we would be diminished by the loss of someone so close.

Already I was discovering, at a whole new level beyond anything I had previously experienced either personally or professionally, the savage power of grief to demotivate and to depress. In the days ahead I found myself relating to the words of C. S. Lewis in his book *A Grief Observed*. He had changed the biblical analogy of marriage as two people becoming "one flesh" to "one ship". Following the loss of his wife Joy, who had died of cancer, he had written:

> *The starboard engine has gone I, the port engine, must chug along somehow till we make harbour. Or rather, till the journey ends.*
>
> *How can I assume a harbour? A lee shore, more likely, a black night, a deafening gale, breakers ahead and any lights shown from the land probably being waved by wreckers.*[12]

Bleak as these cleverly written words may be, they captured the irreparable sense of loss and hovering despair that I was feeling. His take on grief was also very accurate, I felt:

> *Grief still feels like fear. Perhaps, more strictly, like suspense. Or like waiting; just hanging about waiting for something to happen.*
>
> *It gives life a permanently provisional feeling. It doesn't seem worth starting anything. I can't settle down... Up to this I always had too little time. Now there is nothing but time. Almost pure time, empty successiveness.*[13]

As I looked at our children I could see that they too were finding

---

12   C. S. Lewis, *A Grief Observed*, New York: HarperCollins, 2001, pp. 33–4.
13   Lewis, *A Grief Observed*, p. 33.

it hard to settle on anything. All of us stayed up later than usual. Although they were now grown up, they suddenly seemed to me to be much younger and more vulnerable.

Inwardly I vowed to be strong for them, to help them as best I could through uncharted waters. I didn't want them to lose their Dad as well as their Mum.

On the surface, I knew, we had so much to be grateful for – our health, our family, our home, our friends, our common faith, and a supportive church that was allowing us the summer weeks to do whatever we wanted. But what did we want to do? What did we feel like doing? What did we have the energy to do? Clearly, we were all emotionally and physically exhausted.

Yet much as we shared "the permanently provisional feeling", I knew we should not "just hang around waiting for something to happen". We resolved to make some decisions.

The first decision was a very practical one. We decided to go to bed earlier and get out of bed when we woke up rather than lie there thinking and, most likely, sinking into gloom. This proved easier said than done. But getting up, out and on with it was a life-enhancing discipline. Often I wanted to delay the moment when I faced another day without Carol. At the same time I didn't want to stay put because I was all too aware that I was now alone in bed. There were times as I was waking when I would instinctively reach out to cuddle Carol, and then I would groan as the bitter reality kicked in.

We also decided we needed to get some kind of structure in our lives for the immediate future. So for the next few days we would make plans that involved a balance of time inside and outside the home.

We had to learn to spread our wings again. In the weeks leading up to Carol's death I had only been able to pop out for a brisk walk in the neighbourhood. Now it was time for longer walks and talks with family and with friends such as Pete, Linda and Erin, who were still with us. We needed some time to play back the events of recent days and also try to remember so many good times.

Then we would head up to the North-East of England where our friends Ken and Lois Gott suggested we hang out for a couple of weeks while we figured out what to do next. It turned out to be a much better plan than we could have ever envisaged at the time.

Although a Southerner, I had long felt at home in the kingdom of the down-to-earth Geordies and the land of late great Northumbrian Christian giants like Aidan, Bede and Cuthbert. When my Dad died, one of his closest friends, Herbert Harrison, something of a spiritual giant himself, who had pioneered a large church in Newcastle, had taken me under his wing.

Now, although Herbert too had passed on, his daughter Lois, his son-in-law Ken and their family repeated the favour a generation later. Their loving hospitality and the warm embrace of the Metro Church they pastored brought comfort to four wounded souls.

We lost count of the number of people who came up to give us a hug and to tell us how much they were praying for us. I could see how much such love and affirmation meant to the kids. As for me, I was almost overwhelmed.

We stayed in a wonderful large old house in South Shields. The owners, Klaus and Gudrun Lleweling, part of the Metro Church leadership, were away on holiday in Germany. Hearing our news, they had instantly agreed that we should be given the freedom of their family home.

It was the kind of place Carol would have loved, with its Aga and large kitchen and rooms with high ceilings. And it was in the area that provided the backdrop to the poignant Catherine Cookson novels that Carol read so avidly.

Here, away from phone and home, I felt the weight of responsibility, ever so slightly, begin to lift from my shoulders. For the first time in a very long while it felt like we were in a safe place. We could sleep in, read, pray, reflect, watch movies, have some meals together and talk and cry undisturbed.

We made the most of the longer northern summer evenings and took a lot of walks along nearby beaches and cliff-tops. We discovered a secluded smugglers' cave, the atmospheric Marsden Grotto, where we lingered on a terrace watching the waves break, breathing in the pure sea air. I savoured these moments – surprising highs that could so quickly swing back to less surprising lows.

After being around so much sickness and death, we were being reconnected with life. The simple scenes of nature suddenly seemed more vivid than ever. The sea seemed bluer. The grass was greener. The rock-face of the cliffs appeared in high definition. I even had a new appreciation of the shrieking seagulls, while making sure to stay out of their line of fire.

I felt bad that it felt so good. It didn't seem right that we were free to enjoy ourselves when Carol, who had been through so much, could not. Of course, as a pastor I knew how to counsel myself about all this, but that didn't make it any easier to cope with personally.

I just wished Carol was with us. At the same time I knew she would be happy that we were able to at least glimpse a future with some kind of normality.

But what did that look like? There was no script telling us what the next scene should be. So the four of us sat down one sunny morning to have a heart-to-heart and consider our options.

As there were no pressing reasons for any of us to be anywhere particular that summer, we saw no point in trying to rush into a new season of life. So we decided that after returning from the North-East, we would sort out various administrative matters and then we would head off again for a longer break. The rough plan was to try to gain some measure of comfort and healing away from home base, with all its memories, responsibilities and relationships.

My offer of a holiday in the States, as a gift from Carol and me, was readily accepted by the kids. I enjoyed seeing them enthused by the prospect. We agreed to have time out together but also to visit Mike and Linda Peters and other friends. Then we would come back in September ready, hopefully, to get on with studies and careers.

We doubted that it would all work out as neatly as that and I did not want to anticipate whether or not I would feel able by then to resume preaching after a long absence. But at least we had something to look forward to and some positive goals to aim at.

Before we could put this plan into action, however, Lois Gott had a more immediate proposal. A group from their church was about to visit one of the world's biggest churches, Misión Carismática Internacional (MCI) in Bogotá, Colombia. Someone had dropped out and Lois felt that James should go in his place. What did we think?

The suggestion did not appeal to me at all. To have one of my sons travelling to one of the most dangerous countries in the world just after the funeral of his Mum was not what I had in mind at that particular moment. Why, at a time like this, would I want him to make such a trip when foreigners risked being kidnapped, hauled into a jungle, held to ransom or even killed?

But James was not focused on such negative thoughts.

He came to talk to me. He told me that he wanted to go but that he wouldn't leave unless I and his brother and sister felt that he should. So we talked it over. After some reflection and discussion, we each agreed that he should go. I felt we had made the right decision but it was hard to keep out the fear.

James's first call from Bogotá did not entirely reassure me. He happened to be staying at the same hotel as the President-Elect, Álvaro Uribe, a prime target for assassination.

"Dad," he said, trying to cheer me up with some ironic humour, "it's quite safe where we are staying. There are soldiers ringed around the hotel. The bomb squad has got sniffer dogs in reception and I can see a sniper guarding us from the roof."

"Thanks a lot, James," I responded in kind, "that makes me feel a whole lot better."

In just over a week, however, I was able to relax as James and the group arrived back safe and sound. They were full of inspirational and moving tales about a church that had grown from eight members in 1983 to a quarter of a million members by 2002. All this had taken place in a nation bedevilled by drug cartels, terrorism and poverty.

James had clearly been strongly affected by the visit. "Dad," he said, "a lot of people get healed in this church. I saw people get up out of wheelchairs and cry as they told of how pain had suddenly left them.

"Even though I was pleased for them it was hard to watch. I wondered what would have happened if Mum could have come here or if our church was like this church. But one night one of the leaders told how he had taken his seriously ill son to a service, but the next day his little boy died. He told us how heartbroken he was and how he had just cried out for God to heal his heart.

"And then this guy said, 'If anyone here tonight is

heartbroken, God will meet you if you really cry out to him.' So high up in the auditorium I knelt down and started to cry my heart out to God. The moment my knees touched the concrete floor it was like a hand was placed gently over my heart and I felt so warm. I know I am still going to miss Mum so much, but I feel like I have had a healing in my heart."

By the time James had finished telling us his story I was in tears. So too were others when he retold his story. It wasn't just what he said, touching as that was, but the sincerity and mellowness with which he said it.

In the days ahead his lasting sense of peace and new perspective was to be a great support to us. Obviously James still missed his Mum big time, but something had clearly happened to him that had not yet happened to Wes, Mel and me.

No doubt we too could have cried out to God as James had done, but that in itself was a struggle. Mel was just about managing to pray. Wes, who had prayed so long and hard for his Mum, told me he found it too painful to pray. Every time he tried to pray he thought of his Mum. It was too much to deal with. It was to be some long months before he felt able to pray again.

I felt for them. More than ever, I hungered for an intimacy with God that Christians through the ages had spoken of and which I myself had known. But, much as I wanted to, I also was finding it very hard to pray at all. I was glad of a long-established daily habit that kept me focused on God as our Father and his eternal kingdom. Yet I just seemed to be going through the motions of saying the Lord's Prayer and praying in keeping with its various sections. I just couldn't get connected. It was like the receiver was down at the other end.

I found it difficult to read my Bible too. Right now I didn't want to go to any church services. The truth was that I felt emotionally and spiritually spent. I had hit the wall.

I was having an emotional crisis, rather than a crisis of faith. I had experienced too much in my life to doubt that God was real. I also could relate to the words of the venerable Karl Barth, who declared after a lifetime of study that the most profound theological concept he had come across was that "Jesus loves me, this I know, for the Bible tells me so."

For sure, I believed all this. I believed that "all things work together for good for those who love God" (Romans 8:28, NKJV) and plenty of other scriptures that I could rattle right off. But right now it felt like my best friend, who had the power to intervene, had allowed our loved one to be taken out and us to get pretty knocked about. I could not begin to understand it and I did not expect that I ever would.

For all this, I did not feel mad at God and even if I had, I didn't have the energy to rage against Him. I just felt sad; totally, relentlessly sad. At that moment, I was just glad to be able to get away for the summer.

Chapter 10

TIME OUT IN AMERICA

JUST BEING TOGETHER thousands of miles from home with the sun on our backs and wide, open spaces to explore was a reassuring flashback to happier days, albeit with the ever-present awareness that Carol was not with us. Every photo opportunity of us celebrating our visits to landmark sites was also a reminder that there were now four, not five of us lining up for a picture.

Time and again I found myself longing to share a new experience or a beautiful view with Carol and to savour her delight. Once or twice I became so absorbed in the moment that I even turned to address her. Most of all, I just hugely missed being with her and hanging out doing everyday stuff together.

My intention to give the kids a wonderful break after such a gruelling period had a double edge. The more they enjoyed themselves, the more they wished that their Mum was soaking it all up with them.

It was good to see them getting some fun back in their lives, but memories of Mum on previous trips were never far away. Yet the very act of stepping out into new experiences, even with the shakiness of a toddler learning to walk, was to prove pivotal to our ability to move forward into whatever the future held.

Our break in the States, however, was also to heighten our awareness of suffering and prove a source of comfort and strength in ways we could not have anticipated.

The first stop was New York, a great favourite with the kids and me. It was not only poignant to revisit places where we had last been with Carol but also because we were among the early batch of tourists who were returning to the city in the first summer after 9/11.

Hotel rates had been massively discounted and we were staying in a suite just a few blocks from Ground Zero. Visiting the site reduced us all to silence. The gaping hole, far bigger than we had imagined, was not just in the ground but in a nation's heart and in the hearts of thousands of people whose lives and families would never be the same again. All around on nearby sidewalks were makeshift memorials with pictures of loved ones and tributes that were almost too sad to read.

On hearing our English accents total strangers came up to talk to us. They said how much they had appreciated British support in an hour of desperate need and particularly the playing of their national anthem at Buckingham Palace.

They opened up to us as if we were old friends. We gained personal insights into how bravely they or people they knew well were dealing with unimaginable grief. We drew strength from their strength. Some were particularly clear in talking about the comfort they had received from their Christian faith and about their utmost respect for the work of the Salvation Army and many other Christian churches in New York. All this made a deep impression on me and I could see that it had on the kids also.

What also made a deep and shocking impression was a conversation we had with a waiter in a restaurant overlooking the Hudson River and the Statue of Liberty. We had struck up a good rapport with him during the meal but before we left his consuming bitterness about 9/11 came spilling out.

"I am friends with many fire-fighters and their families," he said. "I have been to scores of their funerals. I am so [expletives] angry. If I could, I would go right now to their countries and wipe out every man, woman and child. I would kill every last one of them personally. I want them totally annihilated."

I tried to be sympathetic and said how much we recognized the utter evil of 9/11. I also attempted to say as gently as I could that no matter how much grief any one of us goes through in our lives, surely hate only begets more hate and bitterness just gives rise to greater bitterness. "Eye for an eye, tooth for a tooth!" he spat back.

I didn't want to argue with him but, wisely or not, I found myself responding. "An eye for an eye only ends up making the whole world blind," I replied, quoting Gandhi. "And what about the teaching of Jesus that we should love our enemies and forgive those who have sinned against us?"

Our vengeful waiter was having none of it. He just wanted to rage on. Mel was very upset by this ugliness of spirit and did not want to hear any more of this tirade. She got up from the table and walked a distance away. I told our waiter that I needed to go after my daughter. I said that I hoped he would find some peace, gave him a good tip and left with a heavy heart.

As we all walked back along a promenade we tried to shake off the venom that we had just encountered. As we talked together we concluded that no matter how bad or hard things might be in life, we could not see any future in travelling down a road of grief that would result in such all-consuming bitterness.

Unexpectedly, we were soon to discover another way to cope with great pain and loss when we had a brief visit to Chicago. As we were there over a weekend, we decided to go to a Saturday evening service at a church I had visited once before. I didn't know what the programme was going to be but I thought it would be a positive experience for the kids. I guess I also wanted to be able to slip in somewhere where nobody knew us and gain some insight as to whether God was still on our case. Or put another way, in words spoken to the Hebrew prophet Jeremiah, I wondered if there was "any word from the Lord".

We arrived at Willow Creek Community Church in South Barrington, just outside the city, only to find that there was in fact going to be no "word", at least no word via a sermon. But there, as an anonymous part of the crowd at one of America's largest churches, we heard a message that spoke directly to us.

It came in the form of an interview with a special guest the church had brought in for a series of services that particular weekend. The interviewee was Lisa Beamer, whose husband Todd had died on 9/11 after shouting "Let's roll!" on United Flight 93. Todd was among the group of passengers who wrested control of the plane from hijackers before it reached its intended target, causing it to crash instead in an empty field in Pennsylvania.

The slightly built mother of three young children spoke with great candour and calmness about how her Christian faith had helped her cope with her heartache – what's more, a family heartache exposed to the full glare of the international media. She shared how her own father had died when she was fifteen. She talked about having to break the news to her eldest son, aged just three, that his father, a committed Christian, was never coming back.

I found it difficult yet compelling to listen to someone whose experience of grief was so raw and so recent. At the same time I really wanted to know how she had coped both emotionally and spiritually.

She said that her struggle had been difficult but that the Lord knew on 10 September all that was going to happen. She didn't have to know the reason why. "He's God and I'm not. Who am I to say, 'This plan is not so good here'? But it's tempting sometimes."

Lisa said she talked to the telephone operator who had spoken to her husband minutes before the plane crashed. "Let's roll!" had been his catchphrase. "It was a blessing to me that even in the worst moments of his life, he remained the person that he was. He was able to put himself so freely in the hands of God, to trust and obey."

Lisa was clearly doing that herself. For in a long and searching interview she showed no trace of bitterness or anger, in marked contrast to our troubled waiter.

As Lisa spoke I glanced at the kids to see how they were responding. They were riveted, Mel particularly. I felt I couldn't have planned for more fitting words or a more appropriate young woman to speak to my daughter. Of all the places we could have been, we were where we needed to be at that one particular moment in time.

Similar "coincidences" or "divine appointments" just seemed to happen as we went about the serious business of relaxation. Driving around the tourist spots of Los Angeles with Wes and Mel (James just wanted to rest up), I realized that we were near a famous church that I had read about. This was the West Angeles Cathedral, the home church of Denzel Washington and other Hollywood celebrities. The reputation of this church was such that it merited a positive mention in the *Time Out* guide to LA. On impulse we parked and went to see if we could look around this very obvious landmark in a mostly distressed area.

An office was open and we were quickly made to feel at home by a receptionist. We had not expected to meet the highly regarded and much in demand senior pastor, Bishop Charles Blake. But not only was he on site when we arrived but also, as if on cue, he walked out of an office to greet us.

"Ah, the British are here, the British are here!" he said in an impressively rich voice and with a mischievous grin. Wes and Mel were instantly won over by the warmth of the welcome of this tall, distinguished ambassador of Afro-American Christianity.

We chatted a while about the church but then with a shepherd's insight, Bishop Blake probed to find out why the three of us had wanted to stop by. Such was his fatherly presence that in front of my kids I found myself facing up to the real reason we had gone into the church. Sure, we were curious about the church, but really I was hoping to find some comfort and strength to help us through another day.

I cannot recall what Bishop Blake said but I can vividly remember this great black preacher instinctively reaching his long arms out to a white pastor and his grown-up kids and drawing us into one tight circle for an extended hug. Then he prayed a prayer of such compassion and conviction that I felt as if we had suddenly tapped into undiscovered reserves of healing oil.

The more he prayed with such confidence that God would always be faithful to His children in all circumstances, the more peace seemed to pour over us. The kids felt it too. This was a prayer of someone who appeared to be on particularly intimate terms with the Almighty and who knew how to pray for people who needed help from God.

When we reluctantly said our farewells, we all hugged Bishop Blake. We left with a new sense of peace and well-being. As we drove away it seemed none of us wanted to talk for a while.

A few days later we were to have another, similar encounter with old friends of my late parents. Paul Schoch, a gentle, grandfatherly giant of a man and his wife Margaret, a kindly, grandmother figure, were veteran preachers and missionaries. They were now in their late seventies. They welcomed us like family at their home in Oakland near San Francisco.

Wes, James and Mel were very touched as Paul and Margaret showed them photographs of their happy times with my parents. They told them one fond anecdote after another about their grandfather, who had died before any of them were born, and about their grandmother, who had died when they were young. They also reminisced about Carol and showed them photographs of their Mum and me in the early years of our marriage.

The power of deep roots of family, and friends who are like family, can be very strong at the best of times. At the worst of times we discovered that they had a power to bring a great sense of security. It felt like we had found a family haven on the other side of the world.

Paul and Margaret shared how the long years of friendship had meant that they had mourned the loss of loved ones in our family – first my father, then my mother, eighteen years later, and now Carol. More recently they had also experienced an even closer family loss. Their eldest child, Herb, a much-loved son and father of three children, had only a few months before suddenly dropped dead while doing a household job. He was just fifty-one. There had been no warning and it just seemed completely random and overwhelmingly sad.

As we listened to Paul and Margaret and as each of us shared some of what we were coping with, we had a big family cry together. Getting hugged by Paul was, I imagined, like getting embraced by a big friendly bear. But he and Margaret had clearly also found an eagle-like ability to rise above adversity in their personal lives and in a ministry where they had pretty much seen it all.

I asked him how they managed it. The four of us listened attentively to answers that were simple and profound as well as memorable and moving. Like our previous experiences with Lisa

Beamer and Bishop Blake, they came from people whose faith had been forged in adversity.

"Ever since we were young we have proved that the Lord never leaves us or forsakes us. You just have to trust Him when you can't understand. His love is like a great river. There are many bends in the river and things that we don't foresee, but His great river of love just flows on and on. You must make sure you stay in the river."

As I listened to Paul and Margaret talk I marvelled afresh at the power of living faith and felt great gratitude that our kids could learn from people of such poise and perspective.

I was to do a lot more marvelling as we headed for some real-life rivers, bears and eagles in Yosemite National Park. Here, for a few memorable and carefree days in the spectacularly clean air of the great outdoors, we gazed at awesome mountain views. We looked up at trees that seemed as if they had been around for ever. We tried to fix in our memories the vivid colours and the sheer wild beauty of a countryside to which even the highest-definition camera could not do justice.

More than ever, I found it impossible to believe that everything we were seeing had just fallen so perfectly into place by overwhelmingly unlikely odds of chance. To borrow the memorable phrase of C. S. Lewis, that would be "like upsetting a milk jug and hoping that the way the splash arranges itself will give you a map of London".[14]

And I also reflected that if the wonders of creation indeed indicated a Creator, a possibility acknowledged by many leading scientists, then some words of the psalmist made a lot of sense: "What is man that you are mindful of Him, or the son of man that you visit him?" (Psalm 8:4, NKJV).

---

14 C. S. Lewis, "Rival Conceptions of God" in *Mere Christianity*, New York: Harper Collins, 2001.

Standing small in the vast expanses of Yosemite, I personally had little problem believing that God was great. But was it really true that God was mindful of mere individuals?

Apart from an undeserved grace, I could not fathom why that would be the case. And for sure, I did not expect to understand or explain the countless instances of suffering and pain when God did not seem at all "mindful" of man.

Yet as we continued our break, with its unexpected twists and turns, I felt increasingly that God was trying to show us that He was still watching over us. I could also see that, through the various surprising encounters during our time in the States, each one of our family was stronger in our hearts and faith at the end of our holiday than we had been at the beginning. All this was quietly reassuring. I was not yet sure, however, that I was ready to start preaching again.

This was a subject about which Mike Peters had some very clear ideas, which he shared when we joined his family in St Louis. Towards the end of our holiday he told me that I was going to be the guest preacher at his church on the following Sunday. "This, my friend, is where you get back in the saddle," he said in mid-western no-nonsense cowboy speak.

I had not preached for several months, not since Carol's health had seriously deteriorated. So I felt a degree of nervousness at the prospect of getting back in the pulpit.

As it happened, a passage of Scripture had caught my attention. I thought it would be a relevant first sermon for whenever I recommenced preaching. But I wasn't sure if I could handle it emotionally, especially if I saw others getting emotional. Pete's wife Linda, for example, was still feeling the loss of her dear friend Carol so deeply that she had cried at the sight of an empty seat next to me when we were out to dinner.

In the event, Pete handled it wonderfully as he reintroduced me to the congregation of Christ the King Church in Webster Groves, St Louis. He told them that this was where a new phase of life and ministry was about to begin for me and for our family.

I knew many of the people, as I had preached to them over a number of years. I sensed them willing me on as I got up to speak. In the event there were few dry eyes in the house by the time I finished. But as my American buddy put it, I was back in the saddle and ready to preach this sermon again to our home church when I returned to England.

The title of my talk was "How to stay close to God when He doesn't do what you expect".

Chapter 11

BACK HOME

THE WINDSOR BOYS' School hall, one of the largest venues in the area, was packed on our first Sunday back at our home church. It was inevitably a poignant service for so many.

It seemed strange to be returning. At the same time it was good to be back among hundreds of people that we knew so well. There were also plenty of new faces in the congregation and, as I was soon to discover, some young visitors from the tip of Africa.

It took us a while to reach our seats, as so many people came up to greet us. But for all the smiles and kind words, there was no hiding the concern that people clearly felt for us and no avoiding the pain that Carol would never again be gathering with us and them.

It was nearly a year since Carol herself had spoken and asked us to keep praying for her. The church had faithfully done so, but now there was no Carol and no trite answers.

Carol had been a friend, mentor and mother figure to many. This was our first time together as a church family since the funeral when we were to attempt a walk through our shared grief and into an unknown and uncharted future.

For all the warmth of the welcome expressed in many ways that morning, I was alone with my thoughts as I waited for the moment when I would speak. I wanted to be real in what I would say. I wanted us to face up to the cold and brutal truth that what so many had prayed for had not happened. And I wanted to show that our hope as Christians was not dependent on our feelings and failures or circumstances and challenges.

At first when I stood up, I felt depleted and daunted as the congregation went very quiet. But as I read the opening scriptures I felt a sudden surge of strength and spiritual empowerment.

It was a startling sensation. In an instant I felt a great sense of peace and I soon discovered an unexpected ease of speech. Actually, it was wonderful. It was as if rain had just dropped out of nowhere after a long, long drought.

My theme was the same one that had a not-so-dry run in St Louis. I began my message quoting the passage from the end of Luke's gospel where the resurrected Jesus joined two downcast disciples walking on the road to Emmaus. In their sadness and confusion following the crucifixion, they confided, "we had hoped that he was the one who was going to redeem Israel" (Luke 24:21).

It was the phrase "we had hoped" that stood out to me. For we too had hoped for a very different outcome in response to our prayers for Carol, I said.

> *This passage, and this text in particular, has become
> very meaningful to me personally, as it has, no doubt,
> to other Christians who have found themselves
> caught up in circumstances beyond their control and
> comprehension.*
>
> *Sometimes there are experiences that seem to
> make no sense whatsoever but which totally alter your
> life forever. Hopes and dreams can be shattered in an
> instant.*

*Death, disease, divorce, a betrayal, a rejection,
a vicious verbal or physical attack, among other
dark experiences – each have the capacity to bring
unexpected suffering. Pain and sadness may seem
overwhelming. Questions loom larger than answers.*

*For the non-believer, who regards life as
totally random, all this is only to be expected. For
the Christian, however, who believes in a God who
is all good, all powerful, all knowing and all wise,
there can come even deeper hurt when our actual
experiences do not seem to indicate that God is all, or
any, of the above.*

*Indeed, for Christians who believe in the
reality and possibility of modern-day miracles, it
is particularly hard to accept when we do not see
miracles that we have prayed for with such fervour
and constancy.*

*Such experiences, while undeniably tough are,
however, nothing new. Even the greatest of saints have
experienced times when they were not at all sure what
was going on.*

I said that these disciples on the road to Emmaus were no exception. And yet at their moment of confusion and pain, they made discoveries that stabilized them and turned them around.

Their first great discovery was that Jesus was with them – even when they didn't realize it. I reminded the congregation that the promised presence of the Lord is one of the great recurring phrases of Scripture. I told the church how this had been our experience as a family over the past eighteen months and up to the present moment.

*There are many things that I do not know but I do
know this: the Lord is always with us. Sometimes
we cannot see Him or feel Him, but we do not and
should not rely on our feelings or human perceptions.
For we have God's word and the ministry of the Holy
Spirit to assure us that He is walking with us. And
sometimes He carries us. The Jesus of the Bible is
Emmanuel, God with us. And He is with you and
with me, whatever the times or circumstances.*

I went on to say that some of those times made no sense at all:

*We, as modern-day Christians, sometimes find
ourselves equally perplexed by various experiences and
events. Sometimes we may feel guilty or substandard
in our faith if we admit to this. But the fact is that
there is so much we do not understand.*

*When Billy Graham was asked by family
members of the Oklahoma City bombing victims,
'Why did God let this happen?' he humbly replied, 'I
don't know.'*

*I don't know why a pastor friend of mine still
has his mother aged ninety and father aged ninety-five
when his little daughter drowned in his own back
garden.*

*I don't know why my wife, who had so much to
give and live for, should die at fifty-one after so much
prayer.*

*I can understand why so much of the world
lives in poverty – due to man's greed, violence and
corruption – but I can't understand why one poor
person lives and another dies.*

> *And above all, like the disciples, I can't*
> *understand why God did not save His only Son from*
> *death on the cross. Why did it have to be this way?"*

I said that the crucifixion and resurrection stood at the heart of
the Christian message:

> *God did not send suffering, but He meets us in our*
> *suffering. The position that Jesus outlined to the*
> *disciples, and which Paul taught in the epistles, is that*
> *we are to trust that God knows what He is doing even*
> *when the opposite may seem to be the case. It is in our*
> *sense of loss that the Lord Himself comes to us.*
>
> *It was in the breaking of the bread, symbolizing*
> *the broken body of Christ, that these disciples saw*
> *Him. Brokenness is so often the unexpected key to*
> *closeness with God.*

I could see that these words were finding their mark in the hearts
of the congregation. I encouraged them to allow God to "get to
our wounds" in our time of shared vulnerability and pain:

> *Accept that God's ways are not our ways, but that in*
> *all ways He is working for our good. Don't fight God*
> *on this. Surrender to Him. Be still and know that He*
> *is God.*

As we prayed together, a great calm settled on the congregation.
There was a very real awareness of God's presence in those
moments.

Taking it all in, although I did not know it at the time,
were two sisters and a brother from South Africa. The younger

sister was over visiting for a brief holiday and the elder sister had joined the church during our absence. It was their younger brother who had popped in to see Carol after a game of golf with James.

As the service ended many people came up to greet the kids and me. James, however, seemed anxious to take me aside for a quiet word. I wondered if he was OK after an emotional morning. I need not have worried.

He seemed very enthused about the prospect of inviting his friend and his two sisters to a barbecue that we had planned to have at home with some friends after the service. "Could we let them join us, as they have nowhere else to go?" he asked with new-found levels of pastoral concern. He made them sound like helpless refugees.

"Sure," I said, not altogether clear about why he seemed so keen for three virtual strangers to spend this particular Sunday lunch with us.

An hour or so later I remember beginning to clue in when I saw two very attractive young ladies and their good-looking brother striding across our garden. James introduced the girls to me. I told them to make themselves at home. This proved to be a far more prophetic invitation than I realized at the time.

First impressions seemed favourable all round. The South African girls, coming from a very different cultural background, expressed disbelief that I, as a man, would involve myself in the kitchen. I had to break it to them gently that this was a fairly recent development for me and that I was some way short of being a gastronomic genius.

For my part, I was struck by how naturally each of the three immediately fitted in with us all. They were very relaxed with us and chatted openly. It was as if we had all known each other for a long time.

But who were they? I was to discover that they were the children of a couple who were pastors of a church in Robertson, a small town 100 miles north of Cape Town.

Wilana Erasmus, the eldest of the three, had been the first to make the break from her close-knit church and community back home. She had found it difficult to leave but had been confirmed in her decision to do so after reading some verses from the Bible that had seemed tailor-made for her situation. They were words spoken to Abraham: "Leave your country, your people and your father's household and go to the land I will show you" (Genesis 12:1).

At first she had thought that place might be Canada but doors opened up for her to work as a theatre nurse in England. She found rented accommodation overlooking The Windsor Boys' School. Seeing so many cars arrive on a Sunday morning, she suspected that a church might be meeting there and on investigation quickly found herself a new spiritual home in the UK.

Her brother Drikus (short for Hendrikus) was seven years younger. At eighteen, he had come over for a gap year or two after leaving secondary education and was camping out at his big sister's place. He slotted right in with us, especially when we discovered a mutual interest in rugby.

He soon became a regular visitor, especially when there was international rugby on TV. I did not realize at first the price that I would have to pay for his enthusiasm. On one memorable, and sadly not infrequent, occasion when his beloved Springboks were giving England a hammering, he jumped up in my lounge, pumped the air with his fist, broke the ceiling lights, and landed back in his seat with such force that he broke the sofa. It was impressive how much damage he managed to achieve in one movement and in one moment.

In addition to his talents as a one-man demolition unit, Drikus was also skilled at overseeing barbecues or *braais*, as the South Africans call them. He was in his element socializing with new-found friends.

Vasti, also a nurse like her sister, was the middle child and three years older than Drikus. Although she was just visiting, there was clearly something uncannily familiar about her. For those of us who remembered Carol at the same age as Vasti, the resemblance between them was striking. And from the first moments, the way she fitted into the family made it seem like she had always been part of it.

This did not surprise Margaret Beasley, who was part of our lunchtime group. She kept her counsel at the time but told me later that as she had sat next to Vasti she felt sure that she was talking to James's future wife.

James, it seemed, had similar ideas. He took me aside for a quiet chat. "Dad," he said and paused. "As the girls were chatting with you, it was like I saw the three of you framed in a photograph, and it seemed that you were chatting with your daughters-in-law!"

I was amused by the enthusiastic manner in which James told me this. But I also registered the confident way in which he said it.

"Is this some kind of revelation or is this just a deep personal wish?" I asked him, half seriously and half joking.

"Both!" he answered crisply with his characteristic cheeky smile.

In the next few days before Vasti went back, James tried valiantly not to betray too much of his interest in the second sister. His attempts to appear disinterested were, I thought, somewhat undermined by the way he took every opportunity to be near to Vasti and attach himself to the Erasmus family.

After Vasti had flown back and Drikus had continued his travels in the UK, the links continued to build with the "Erasmai", as I christened them. Mel struck up a friendship with Wilana, who became a regular guest at our Sunday lunch table.

Wes, however, did not seem so keen on having a relatively unknown visitor around the house so often at a time of emotional family readjustment. He remarked, as Mel later reminded him in very different circumstances, "She's your friend, not my friend."

Wes had a good point. The early weeks after Carol's death passed uncertainly and slowly as we tried to map out some kind of new routine in our lives. Running a home threw up new challenges. There were many times when I found myself wanting to ask Carol where something was.

The kids and I took it in turns to shop and to cook. But as much as we all pitched in to make everything seem as normal as possible, there was a hovering sense of sadness and dislocation. It seemed like we were in a holding pattern waiting for permission to land and get our feet on firm ground.

James and Mel began to make tentative plans for simultaneous gap years. Wes was busy applying for selection to train as a barrister.

I started to get back up to speed with church life and concentrated on preparing a preaching series on discovering hope beyond your hurt. It was based on studies from the book of Ruth and was entitled "What becomes of the broken-hearted?" – a title taken from Jimmy Ruffin's old song.

Years later, I still receive positive feedback from this teaching series, which was crafted in the midst of our own search for an answer to that question.

The story from this little Old Testament book spoke to me well before I preached it to anyone else. It gave me hope because it started with bereavement and bitter experience but ended with unexpected and cascading blessings both in the immediate and distant future. Over the next few weeks and months we slowly began to perceive that unexpected blessings were indeed coming our way too.

Gert and Lina Erasmus, Dad and Mum of the Robertson Three, visited us and immediately treated us as if we were part of their family. They thanked us for looking after their kids and said that they wanted to help us in any way they could. They invited us to stay with them for a break in South Africa.

I politely thanked them and gave a non-committal answer. Afterwards, however, James told me that Drikus was going home in a few weeks' time and he very much liked the idea of going with him to play some golf and hang out in the sun.

"Also," he said, getting to what we both knew was a compelling reason for the trip, "it would be good to meet Vasti again."

James was nothing if not thorough when he put his mind to a particular goal. I could see that he had his mind set on investigating whether there was a continuing spark between him and Vasti. Mel said she would love to come. Wes, however, needed to stay behind.

I was torn about whether or not to go. I could see that the idea of a break, especially with some of the kids, could do us all a lot of good. But it was a big step into the unknown. In the end I decided to call Gert. I asked if I could speak frankly about what was going on in my mind. He said he was fine with that.

"Gert, thanks for the invite, but why would I come at one of the most vulnerable times in my life, to a country I have never visited, to stay for a holiday with people I hardly know?" I asked.

"Since you have been open with me, I will be open with

you, Wes," Gert replied. "You have really been on our hearts as a family after all you have been through. We believe God has put it on our hearts to do what we can to look after you. Besides, we have a lot of fun as a family and we will give you a good time. So just come over."

I thanked Gert for being so helpful and said I really appreciated his kindness. I said I would call him back in a few days.

When I put the phone down, I felt unsettled. But at the same time I thought we should go. So I called Gert back. "We're coming to South Africa," I announced. I put the phone down and was surprised at the sense of excitement and anticipation that I felt.

When I told Melody she enthusiastically endorsed the idea and started packing the biggest case she could find. Wes agreed, with some reluctance, that he would keep an eye out for Wilana while our family met her family. James just grinned at his brother's discomfort and, not least, at the prospect of an imminent reunion with Wilana's dark-haired sister.

Chapter 12

A NEW WORLD OPENS UP

W E WOKE UP TO brilliant sunshine near the end of a long night flight from cold, old London. The whole of the Cape Peninsula, with its ocean-surrounded mountain range and exotic vegetation, sparkled below us like one of South Africa's famed diamonds.

As we came in to land it was like a scene from *The Lion, the Witch and the Wardrobe*, only in reverse. Instead of stepping through a wardrobe into a land of winter, we stepped out of a jet plane into a summer paradise.

It was just after 6 a.m. on 15 November 2002 when James, Mel and I walked on to African soil for the first time. The heat hit us so hard, even so early in the morning, that we looked at each other and laughed. What a contrast to so many recent grey days at home.

We were glad that we'd made the decision to come even as we collected our baggage. But greater delights were in store. James was trying to focus on one of them as the Arrivals door opened up and we looked for our hosts.

They were standing right in front of us. Both were dressed in shorts and casual shirts. Their very tanned limbs made me feel like a very overdressed white English missionary lacking only a pith helmet and compass.

Gert greeted us like long-lost friends. Vasti was affecting

interest in all of us too and welcomed us warmly enough. But when she and James greeted, as I could not help noticing in my peripheral vision, it seemed to me more like an embrace than a hug. It was just a few seconds too long – long enough to give the game away.

I was therefore not entirely surprised that when it came to allocating us and our luggage to different cars, Vasti generously offered, "You can travel with me, if you like, James." Mel, clearly amused by this turn of events, reconciled herself to an enthralling ride with the two Llads. As it happened, the entire journey to the family home was nothing short of a rejuvenating introduction to a whole bright new world.

One of our first stops was at Bloubergstrand beach with its spectacular views of Table Mountain, so beloved of photographers and artists. Almost within touching distance was Robben Island where, for eighteen harsh years out of twenty-seven in captivity, Nelson Mandela demonstrated his legendary resilience in adversity.

Even though the story was so well known, I was moved, standing on that beach, as I reflected that someone who had been so near yet so far from freedom for so long, could emerge with such a remarkable lack of bitterness. Without that nobility of spirit, I doubted that we would be safely walking around in the new rainbow nation and enjoying its stunning beauty.

Even the N1 motorway out of Cape Town to Paarl, the Afrikaans name for a pearl of a location, was a sight to behold. For mile after mile the central reservation was an explosion of colourful flowers and bushes.

Mel and I had never been to a place which created such an outstanding first impression. James, we later discovered, felt the same way, although at that point, as he sat close to the lovely Vasti, he would have probably said that anywhere was exceptional.

The landscape now opening up before us was a picture-book scene of fertile green valleys, pine and oak forests, vine-covered hills and farms with their characteristic white, thatched, Cape Dutch homes. Signposts to Stellenbosch and Franschhoek indicated that we were in the centre of one of the most fruitful wine-lands in the world.

Gert delighted in pointing out a variety of sights to us, some of them definitely unexpected. He was amused to see our startled reactions as baboons suddenly appeared on the mountain road before us. "Would you like to stop?" he asked, revealing his unique brand of humour. "There are leopards round here too."

Our preference, strangely enough, was to keep moving and on through the original Huguenot Tunnel, a clue to the area's history as a refuge for French Protestant Christians fleeing the brutal persecution of Louis XIV in the late 1600s.

Emerging from the tunnel, we could not get out our cameras quickly enough as the spectacular sights of the Du Toitskloof Pass burst into view before us. We stopped at a little lodge, craning our necks, to marvel at high mountain peaks, craggy cliff faces and dramatic waterfalls that towered over the pass.

I felt oddly comforted looking at these massive rocks but I couldn't figure out why. Maybe it was simply the utter beauty of the place that was getting to me, after an ugly season of suffering.

Then I remembered the passage of Scripture that had first come to me so strongly and incongruously at Hammersmith Hospital in London: "I lift up my eyes to the hills – where does my help come from? My help comes from the Lord, the Maker of heaven and earth."

At that moment, as I looked up in wonder, the words of

Psalm 121 hit home with a new force. God was still keeping us steady and watching over us.

The thought of God being with us in every situation and season of life was further impressed on me as we came down from the mountain pass into the more lush pastures of the Breede River Valley. This valley was fertile both naturally and spiritually. Its business centre, Worcester, had once been the epicentre of a major Christian revival. Its name also indicated Britain's historic influence in South Africa.

There was, in every sense, so much to take in as we continued on our last leg of the journey, a forty-five-minute drive along the R60 through desert-like country more reminiscent of a spaghetti western than Africa.

Our first sight of Robertson, home of the Erasmus clan, was stunning. It spread out before us at the heart of a pretty valley and was surrounded by mountains on all sides. It may not have literally been a land of milk and honey but it was certainly an enchanted territory of wine and roses.

There were vineyards everywhere and their global influence could be found even in our local supermarkets back home. Many of the fifty wine producers, including famous names like Graham Beck, Bon Courage, Van Loveren Excelsior, De Wetshof and the Springfield Estate, had won international acclaim. The public roads around the area were flanked with mile after mile of red and yellow roses.

As we came down a hill into Robertson we seemed to have been transported back at least half a century to a classic one-horse town. Actually, first appearances were deceptive, as Robertson was a centre of the horse-breeding industry in the Western Cape. And if its wide main street, with its imposing white Dutch Reformed church and landmark steeple, often looked sleepy and deserted, this was because so many people worked and lived just out of town on the many farms.

The black community, just over a decade after the fall of apartheid, also lived just out of the centre in some very basic housing in the *Nquebella*, while the brown community were mainly congregated in other outlying areas.

For all these divisions, of which we were later to become more aware, there was a feeling of peace and tranquillity in a town which was founded in 1853. It was named after a highly influential Scottish Dutch Reformed Church minister, Dr William Robertson, in recognition of his long ministry in the all-round care of people of all races and backgrounds.

Right now, though, we were in the care of another locally well-regarded minister, and Gert duly brought us to our promised place of refuge. The Erasmus home, a deceptively spacious one-level building, had its own spectacular vista, as it looked out directly on to well-watered school fields and the Alpine-like contours of the Langeberg Mountains.

Lina greeted us with characteristic enthusiasm. So too did Erasmus family friend Elsie, who had worked with them for many years. She adopted us as her own from the first moment, just as she had the Erasmus kids.

Their pictures were all over the house. There were school portraits on the walls, fun family snapshots held by magnets on the fridge and framed pictures on the piano. The Erasmus kids, unlike our own family, had stuck with their practices and were now all very accomplished pianists, as my mother had been. Drikus was also a gifted guitarist. What's more, all of them could really sing. Little did we realize it at the time, but the music was coming back into our lives.

The whole atmosphere of the Erasmus family and home seemed familiar. As our families sat down together for the first dinner, it all seemed very natural. It struck me that our kids had experienced a very similar Christian upbringing, though continents apart.

It did not strike me as significant that I had two sons and a daughter and Gert and Lina had two daughters and a son. With hindsight, I am sure that Carol would not have regarded this as entirely coincidental.

James was certainly seriously weighing up the possibility of at least one partnership, as he had plenty of chances to get to know Vasti in the context of family gatherings. One evening he came to my room for a chat. "Dad," he said, "I wanted to come here to see if there was really something in this. But now I'm sure. I have found my wife. What do you think?"

"I think, James, that she is lovely and that you should go for it. Just pick your moment to talk to her," I replied and agreed with him to pray some more about this over the coming days.

Over the next week James took every opportunity to be with Vasti. Her younger brother Drikus, who had belatedly joined us from England, was initially at a loss to discern why his English mate was no longer so eager to go out on the golf course with him.

James decided that it would be a good idea to get to know more about what Vasti was really like by climbing Table Mountain with her. They chose one of the tougher routes up the front face of the mountain under the cable car. Vasti later confided to me that she thought that this would be a good opportunity to test the mettle of the town boy from England. She remembers teasing him, "James, you are going to need to keep up with me and I am not going to wait for you."

James, drawing on the competitive experiences, if not the previous fitness levels of his rowing days, had no intention of lagging behind. He made it a point of honour to disguise his breathlessness and was determined not to ask for a break, "even though I was pushed hard to keep up with Vasti".

He casually consented when she suggested that they have a brief rest to admire the scenery on the way up. He felt that all the views before him were indeed highly satisfactory.

When they reached the top after four and a half hours, James concluded that the only gallant thing to do was to give Vasti a kiss to say well done. This apparently was a breach of local cultural protocol and Vasti recalls thinking, "James what are you doing? We are just friends." The lady concedes, however, that she did not protest too much at the time.

Several days later, Vasti was no longer confused, as James took the plunge at a holiday spa in Montagu near Robertson and asked her to go out with him. The two of them sat alone against the backdrop of an illuminated mountain under a starry African sky. James's opening words, however, were not the stuff of romantic movies.

Instead he chose to use some lines from the film *Dumb and Dumber*, knowing that Vasti too was a Jim Carrey fan. "What's the chance of a guy like me getting together with a girl like you?" James asked.

Vasti laughed and played along. "About one in a million," she replied.

James grinned and countered with, "So you're saying there is a chance!"

At this point, Vasti said, she took James's hand because "he was clearly nervous. He was talking really fast and babbling a lot!"

The next morning James woke Drikus, who was sharing a room with him. James was highly amused to tell him, "I kissed your sister last night!" Drikus apparently nearly fell out of his bed with shock.

Mel, meanwhile, was highly amused to see her brother

so besotted and thought that the whole trip was one highly enjoyable adventure. She was basking not only in the sun but in the whole experience.

I remember walking with her along wide avenues encircled by mountains and lined with almost intoxicatingly beautiful mauve and purple jacaranda trees that were in full bloom. With little traffic around, she stood with outstretched arms in the middle of the road and did a spontaneous 360-degree twirl as if auditioning for *The Sound of Music*.

"This has got to be one of the best places in the world," she said. I was touched by her happiness. It was so good to see her so carefree again for the first time in a long while.

We were to experience many other happy firsts on our Cape odyssey. Not only did we feel at home with a new family, but we were also hospitably welcomed to an extended family of church friends.

Pat Paulsen (a former Robertson rugby captain) and his wife Elaine, Philip Swaart (a former Boland forward) and his wife Anna-Marie, and Gher Rabie (a former Western Province player) and his wife Riette had been among the first church members who made us feel welcome. The initial warmth, however, was soon unexpectedly tested.

We had not realized that Robertson had a strong Afrikaner presence and that Afrikaners, with long memories of ruthless treatment by the British in the Boer War, had no great love for the English *rooineks* (rednecks) whose untanned skins burned in the South African sun. They liked nothing better than to see their national rugby team pulverize the English.

It so happened that shortly after our arrival the Springboks were playing the ancient enemy England in what should have been a keenly contested rugby international back home at Twickenham. To my initial pleasure and then creeping embarrassment as we watched the game at Pat's house with our new-found friends, England humiliated the Springboks with a record 53–3 thumping. At home, of course, I would have jumped for joy. Right now I wondered if we should head for cover or at least lie low for a few days.

My unease was compounded when Gert said that he wanted me to preach to his Springbok-loving congregation the very next morning. And so it came to pass that an Englishman stood to be introduced to a particularly quiet congregation comprising many burly, not to say huge, farmers whose arms were uniformly crossed.

I decided on a bold, if potentially foolhardy, approach. "I want to thank you so much for your welcome, especially after the events of yesterday. You are truly Christian people. It is wonderful that you would take us English in at such a time. It just shows what a great and generous spirit you have. For sure, this must be a Christian church, that you so quickly exhibit such a spirit of forgiveness…"

At this point Pat Paulsen, sitting right in front of me, pretended to be offended. He put his hand up and shouted "Stop!" The congregation laughed at this interruption, which I had imagined would not be long in coming, and everybody noticeably relaxed.

Then, in all seriousness, I thanked them for making us feel at home and told them why we so much appreciated their warmth. Once more I spoke on the theme, "How to stay close to God when He doesn't do what you expect".

I shared, frankly, some of the episodes that we had been through and said how our time in South Africa was further evidence of how God continues to walk with us even when we are at our most vulnerable.

I felt a strong connection with this congregation, as if I was with my home crowd. Something was happening with them too in the way they responded that morning. I could see that many of them were moved by my message and by the time we prayed, even some of the big guys had tears in their eyes. More than ever before, I was discovering how much healing of the heart was a universal need.

I could not quite factor all that we were experiencing or why we were in South Africa, but I sensed that we were somehow being undergirded in our mourning and also being guided into a whole new life and a network of new relationships. This trip had offered a hopeful glimpse into the future, certainly as far as James and Vasti were concerned. All this was a considerable comfort as we headed back to the dark and chill of England and our first Christmas without Carol.

Chapter 13

STRUGGLING TO HAVE A MERRY CHRISTMAS

A s Christmas approached we tried to keep as many family traditions as we could. Mel led the way in this, trying to retain her Mum's feminine touch in the home. I was despatched as usual to buy a suitable tree. But dressing it was a tougher challenge.

This was one of Carol's favourite tasks and she had carefully selected decorations from various countries we had visited. Mel usually teamed up with her Mum and together they found a suitable place for everything.

This year I helped Mel take the various items out of the box and fix them on the tree. I felt a very inadequate substitute and I think both of us really wanted to ask Carol if we had done the job right. It was reassuring in one way to be able to use Carol's hand-picked decorations, but neither Mel nor I trusted ourselves to say much to each other.

I could see that Mel and the boys were each trying to appreciate all that we had going for us and make the most of Christmas. But it was the seemingly little things which often betrayed the inner tension and the sadness that everyone was struggling with.

Mel, for instance, tried to reprise her Mum's special diet-busting chocolate, cream and raspberry roulade. She got out her

Mum's instructions but somewhere along the line she missed out an ingredient. In the event it tasted fine but its presentation left something to be desired. We were upset to see how disproportionately distressed Mel was, as we recognized that the collapsed state of the cake only highlighted to her the keenness of the loss of her mentor and best friend.

I tried to be as cheerful as possible but I knew that I was not convincing my family. Christmas was tipping me into a state of turmoil that I was finding hard to control. I knew it was still early days for even an initial adjustment to bereavement. But nearly six months on from Carol's passing, and just a short while after our very special time in South Africa, I thought that I might have gained a greater sense of equilibrium. Instead I just felt like crying my eyes out.

I pretty much did, unexpectedly, at the Royal Albert Hall in London. The kids and I and some family friends had kept up another of our traditions by taking our annual trip to hear *The Messiah* performed by leading soloists, a famous orchestra and a 500-voice choir.

In happier circumstances Handel's classic had often stirred me. But this year, as I sat high up in a darkened concert hall and looked down at the beautifully lit stage, the music and the words of Scripture released in me a pent-up flood of tears.

In particular, it was a phrase from the prophet Isaiah that touched a need deep within me: "Surely He has borne our griefs and carried our sorrows." As these words were sung with such professional excellence, my mind focused on the raw, ugly, awful events of the crucifixion where Jesus suffered and died to save the world from evil, death and hell.

All this I knew and, like countless other recipients of divine grace, I never ceased to be amazed by it. It was the heart of the gospel. But something more struck me now. The promised

Messiah was not just our bearer of sin, sickness and shame, He also took on Himself our griefs and carried our sorrows. I knew I was struggling big time to carry a load that daily seemed harder to bear. But now I had a glimpse of "the Man of Sorrows" who had already made provision for all who grieved.

I heard no voice from heaven, just the massed voices of the choir. But I felt like the Lord Himself was drawing close to me in that famous hall and saying, "Why are you carrying your grief? I have already carried it. Stop struggling. Let me bear the load."

I was grateful that no one could see me but there was no stopping the tears. When I left the Royal Albert Hall later that evening I felt a whole lot lighter. For sure, I knew we would all still need a lot more healing of the heart, but an oppressive weight had definitely lifted.

I determined to do my best to share the good news of Christmas with as many people as I could, especially with those who, for one reason or another, found the season of great joy a time of sadness and emptiness. So on Christmas Eve we made our way back up the steps of Windsor's Parish Church where we had last gathered for Carol's funeral. The local Anglicans had kindly let us use the building for our Christian family service. I felt the poignancy of the occasion for a moment as I tentatively walked up the steps. I wondered whether I had made a big mistake and should have asked someone else to take the service. But my spirit began to lift as I walked in, to be greeted by the buzz of a very full congregation that was gathering.

The atmosphere in the building that evening was really something. The music, the singing and the congregational worship resonated with joy and hope. The words of familiar carols struck me with fresh force and relevance for a broken world. It did me a power of good just to be in one of a vast number of congregations around the world who were celebrating the Saviour's birth. That I was able to once more speak about such good news was an added bonus.

The congregation grew silent as I spoke of how the Christmas message assumed a new depth of meaning for us as a family. At the end of the service I felt a peace that was to comfort me through the Christmas break. The kids too drew a lot of strength from our time together as a church.

On Christmas morning we had breakfast with a few friends that the kids had invited over. Mel particularly had wanted Ilona and Sarah Albrecht to join us. They were two sisters who were part of the church. They too were trying to get back on their feet after the deaths of their Dad and Mum. It was a source of mutual comfort that we could all be together.

As the day went on other friends, both longstanding and more recent, came to join us. In the latter category was Wilana, who was experiencing her first Christmas away from her family in South Africa. She was feeling very homesick. She told me that, although she knew it was impossible, she had half wished and half prayed that she could meet and hug someone from her own family.

She had to make do with phone calls home, although James was hogging the line speaking to her sister. When he finally put the phone down and rejoined the rest of the human race, he too was longing to hug a particular member of the Erasmus clan. He was clearly feeling the distance between England and the tip of Africa.

When he told me this I tried to be as measured as I could in my response. I was relieved that he did not detect a glint in my eye. For I knew that very soon some good news was coming his and Wilana's way.

Two weeks previously I had the sudden thought that I should do something that would shorten the gap between

James's and Vasti's previous and next meetings. I also wondered what Carol would have suggested about helping to smooth out the path of true love for a son who needed to spend more time with his future wife. I had a pretty shrewd idea that she would have wanted us to "make a plan", as the Afrikaners say.

So I had made a private call to Vasti. "Are you working after the Christmas holiday?" I asked, knowing that she was spending Christmas with most of her family in South Africa.

"I am free for a week, as it happens," she said, intrigued.

"Well, I have a deal to put to you. If you will promise me to say nothing about this, I will fly you to England for that week. What do you say?"

"Is this some kind of a joke?" Vasti asked guardedly.

"No, I'm serious. How about it?"

At this point in our conversation, Vasti let out a high-pitched sound that convinced me she had agreed to the proposed deal.

So after her South African Christmas, she kept her end of the bargain. As James put the phone down to Vasti, she wished him good night without giving anything away. Then she boarded her plane for an evening flight to England.

The next morning I got up early and left the house without disturbing anyone. Vasti came through Immigration quickly and greeted me with a big hug. We both laughed at our conspiracy of surprise and could hardly wait to spring it as we drove back home through the gathering light.

We crept into the house quietly and made our way to James's room. I put the light on and he uttered a low groan and pulled the duvet over his head. At this point Vasti sat on the bed and started singing quietly over James the famous Frankie Valli song, "You're just too good to be true, can't take my eyes off of you."

James was too befuddled to appreciate the reality of what was happening. Vasti and I looked at each other with amusement as we waited for his reaction.

Slowly he pulled the duvet down, observed Vasti and looked quizzically at me. Then he pulled the duvet back over his head and settled down for some more sleep.

Vasti laughed at his disorientation. "James, it's me, Vasti! Is this the way you greet me?"

James's head slowly re-emerged. Without saying a word he just pointed at Vasti. It took a few more seconds of staring at Vasti before he managed to stammer, "It can't be you. You're in Africa!"

"Not any more," said Vasti. "I have just flown in and your Dad came to get me."

James's face was indeed a picture of wonder and delight as the penny dropped. Finally he reached up and gave Vasti a massive hug and kiss.

After more hugs, explanations and laughter we made a plan to get Wilana to join us for a breakfast get-together. We all assembled waiting for her arrival, with Vasti sitting in a chair opposite the door.

We thought we should really make the most of the moment. So we had the video camera ready and as Wilana came into our lounge, we put on a soundtrack of South Africa's soulful national anthem. Wilana looked very quizzical and then totally bewildered as she suddenly spotted her sister smiling at her. For a few seconds we thought we had overdone the surprise, as the colour drained from Wilana's face. Then Vasti got up to greet her sister and Wilana's half-prayer/half-sigh was answered in a welter of shrieks, tears and laughter.

When we eventually sat down to breakfast I had the same sense of a family gathering as I had experienced in Robertson. James and Vasti looked very much a couple but Wilana too seemed very much part of the picture. This was good for Mel, who was happy to see the female presence increasing in the home. She got on well with the two Erasmus girls and was very happy to have them around as we hung out together over the post-Christmas holiday.

Wes was not altogether comfortable with this instantly cosy arrangement. His opinion had not changed from the time he had told Mel that "Wilana is your friend, not mine."

He had fulfilled his duties of looking out for Wilana when we were in South Africa and had taken her out for dinner. But there was no indication that the arrangement was anything more than a sociable meeting between the siblings of a couple who were going out together. Wilana recalled that Wesley was "pleasant but both parties seemed relieved that the duty of oversight and being overseen had been performed and that the night had come to closure."

Wes's main focus over the long English winter break was to act as host of a reunion of friends from the London School of Economics. They were staying in the nearby house of a church friend who was away for the holiday. This high-spirited group had flown in from various parts of the world: the States, Italy, Argentina and Norway. Since their graduations many had gone on to well-connected careers and various political and diplomatic roles.

It was a comfort for our family to meet up with them all, as they had been like big brothers and sisters to each of the kids. They were very kind towards me and I could see how much they missed their "English Mum".

One evening I decided to launch out and have them all back to share another meal together around our family dining table as we had done so many times before. In the event we needed to use another table also, as there were eighteen of us, all told. I had never cooked for so large a group but with help from the family and Vasti and Wilana, we pulled off a four-course dinner. There were no recorded complaints and all appeared healthy afterwards. Although I missed Carol keenly, not least her presence in the kitchen, I felt empowered to have done something I had never done before.

Everyone got on so well, even though we were such a varied group around the tables – Christians, a Muslim, atheists and agnostics. I gave a spontaneous and informal after-dinner talk, paying tribute to Carol and sharing some of my discoveries about love, life, faithfulness, marriage, suffering and the profound difference between personal faith and empty religion. I wished them success in their lives and assured them, to laughter, that whether or not they believed in Him, I regularly prayed to God for them. My informal talk was warmly received and led to many very honest and heartfelt discussions.

The Erasmus girls were taking all this in. The LSE young women were quick to make their assessment of the South African sisters. James was warmly and publicly congratulated on his choice. Privately, however, the LSE ladies, notably the South Americans, took Wes aside for a big-sisterly chat:

"Wes, we have been spending time with Wilana. Listening to her is like listening to you. You have so much in common. Plus she's beautiful. She's just perfect for you! What are you waiting for?"

Wes, who I noticed had gradually been more open to Wilana's presence over the Christmas break, agrees that from this moment on he began to consider the sister of his future sister-in-law in a whole new light.

Early in January, with the light of romance shining ever more brightly in the eyes of James and Vasti, his South African beauty reluctantly returned home, the LSE group scattered around the globe and we tried to focus on a New Year.

I now fully re-entered pastoral duties and threw myself into preaching, as I was drawing strength in a new way from the Bible. In a New Year's message I considered the story of Abraham, who had gone on a great journey with God into the unknown. I shared how we, as a family, had been "moved completely out of our comfort zones". At the same time as we had moved forward, we were also making many new and positive discoveries, including the unfolding blessings of our time in South Africa. I challenged the church to be "a willing, mobile, flexible, obedient people", even if it meant taking decisions that seemed "scary".

A week later, mindful of the brokenness that we had experienced as a family and as a church family, I gave some applications from the example of Nehemiah, who had led the way in the reconstruction of Jerusalem after its destruction by the Babylonians. My theme was "It's time to rebuild".

I spoke of how we needed the help of God as we sought to face up to many contemporary needs – the need to rebuild individual lives, the need to rebuild family life, the need to rebuild the role and influence of the Christian church, particularly in the West, and the need to rebuild society.

Within a month I was to learn a great deal more about meeting each of these needs in a country that knew all about chaos and brokenness. It was the source of 85 per cent of the world's drug trade but it was also the place where James had experienced such healing of his heart. Now he was insisting, "Dad, you must go to Colombia. You are going to find help there." With some considerable reluctance, I finally promised him that I would make the long journey to South America.

Chapter 14

HEALING AND ROMANCE IN BOGOTÁ

O UR ARRIVAL IN BOGOTÁ in January 2003 came fully equipped with all the safety features that James had spoken of on his earlier trip. Armed soldiers were on hand to greet us and security was tight. All of our group, including the kids and myself and fellow church members, were given strict instructions to stay together and to follow our guides.

The host church threw a protective cordon around us in the form of a protocol team that met us inside the customs area at the airport. They then proceeded to monitor us continually throughout our stay.

Bogotá, Colombia's capital city, which is situated over 8,500 feet above sea level at the geographical centre of the country, was a prime target in the ongoing nationwide struggle between government forces and Marxist FARC guerrillas. Over 40,000 people had died in the decades-long drug-fuelled war. In the 2002 elections, presidential candidate Ingrid Betancourt had been taken hostage while campaigning.

The election of President Álvaro Uribe, with the support of many church groups, including the massive MCI church, had already started to bring change. Bogotá was safer than it had been for some time, we learned. But it was still vulnerable to terrorist atrocities and kidnappings. The British Foreign Office was still issuing warnings about the dangers and advising against travelling to Colombia. You could feel the tension, for sure. My first and not wholly fanciful impression was that we had landed in a lawless Wild West world where gunslingers could loom into view at any moment.

We were instructed to have no contact with any of the crowds that jostled round the exit to the main airport terminal and were swiftly taken in a hired coach to our hotel. Our group was subdued as we witnessed the heavy army presence along most of the route through commercial areas. Nervous-looking young men cradling machine guns stood at most intersections. Some of the younger members of our party, however, treated it all as a big adventure, fancying themselves as budding Jack Ryans, the Tom Clancy character played by Harrison Ford in the thriller *Clear and Present Danger*.

As our bus turned down one particularly narrow street it was all too easy to imagine shadowy figures on the rooftops suddenly unleashing on us shoulder-held rockets. I began to wish I hadn't watched the movie and reflected that maybe I should have taken more notice of warnings by the British Foreign Office after all.

I was therefore relieved when we made it without incident to our hotel, guarded as it was by a fairly concentrated presence of soldiers. For the next week we only came and went under escort. On no account were we allowed to wander off on our own.

James was showing us around our temporary home with the confidence of a veteran traveller to Colombia. He was eagerly anticipating our reactions to our first visit to the Misión Carismática Internacional (MCI) church.

This was to prove a totally new experience of church. For a start, it gathered in multiple services at the 18,000-seat coliseum in a prominent part of the city. The church also held regular services next door at the 46,000-seat El Campin soccer stadium, home to the national team.

Seeing crowds line up to gain entry to a Christian service under the protective gaze of armed troops and elite military units in full combat gear was quite a sight. As we entered, a conference session was in full swing. The roar of the crowd as they prayed hit us with an almost physical intensity.

It felt like we had been transported to the middle of a joyful fiesta as Christians from across Latin America worshipped God with fervent singing, the waving of colourful banners, a full-on band and a dance troupe with scores of energetic young people. It would have been heart-attack territory for church traditionalists, but for all the sour jibes about "happy clappy" religion, I thought that what I was witnessing had a whole lot more life and passion than what we Westerners often regarded as "normal" Christianity.

The atmosphere in that first service alone was worth all the hassle of travelling to Colombia and adjusting to its sobering daily realities. I was not the only one to feel an immediate sense of peace and well-being. Subsequent services only confirmed first impressions. I could see why James had wanted me to come.

I felt a long way from home but also as if, in some strange way, I had come home. The Colombian church's unashamed declaration and celebration of the Christian gospel in all its profound simplicity reminded me of the many vibrant Sunday evening evangelistic services that my father had led in my youth.

So too did the confident call to all-out commitment if you intended to be a true follower and disciple of Christ. This struck me as a marked contrast to so much watered-down Western Christianity which seemed so obsessed with fitting in with the post-modern world rather than being a light to the world.

I thought Carol, with her keen sensitivity to what was real, would have loved it all and I missed her all the more. Sometimes, being in such a great crowd made the loneliness even more intense. I wondered what I was doing, sitting day after day on tiered stone seats in this distant and dangerous land. But I felt sure that she would have been very pleased that the kids and I were being exposed to such a life-giving environment.

Increasingly, as I soaked in the atmosphere and listened to the inspiring teaching, I felt as if I was being inwardly replenished. I began to glimpse that I had, in the prophet Jeremiah's words, "hope and a future", even though I had little clue what that might look like. I took comfort also from the fact that the senior pastor of the church was a very vivid example of great recovery after great setback.

From the first I was very taken with the normality and sincerity of Pastor César Castellanos and his family. His wife Claudia was not only co-pastor but also a senator in the Colombian parliament. Their four daughters were all very committed Christians.

They all seemed close and relaxed together. All of them, even the youngest daughter Sarah, then ten, would preach or speak at various times. Actually, I thought the ten-year-old was one of the best speakers of the whole conference.

But for all their evident poise, they had certainly been through some very tough times together. On 25 May 1997, after a Sunday morning service, they were travelling to a restaurant to celebrate the thirteenth birthday of one of the girls, Lorena. As they stopped at traffic lights, a motorcycle pulled up and the passenger pulled out a gun. The pastor was shot five times and his wife took a bullet that ended up two inches from her heart. Although the daughters were not hit, they were covered in their parents' blood and broken glass. They were in shock at the horror that had so dramatically overtaken them.

Claudia recovered quickly but for ten days the life of César hung in the balance. For a year the family relocated to America for physical and emotional healing. In this time Pastor César, as he was known, wrote a book called *Dream and You Will Win the World*. Then the Castellanos family courageously returned to continue their ministry in Colombia.

I did not imagine that I would meet the senior pastor of one of the world's largest churches. The demands on Pastor Castellanos's time were considerable and the security around him was tight. But thanks to a Scottish pastor friend, Jimmy Dowds, the kids and I were given the opportunity to meet him.

It was well beyond 11 p.m. when his security team let us through into his office. When he arrived, some moments later, there were several people waiting to be introduced to him. His warmth towards each one of them was the first thing I noticed.

Around five foot five inches tall and very trim, he cut a sharp figure in his smart business suit. But his manner was very fatherly. I sensed the kids relax as he moved towards them with smiles and gave each of them a Latin American hug. The rapport he struck up with them was instant. He seemed to have all the time in the world as he welcomed them and asked them about themselves.

When he came to me, he greeted me like an old friend. He had been well briefed about our story. "I am so sorry to hear the news about your wife," he said quietly through the interpreter. "Is there anything I can do to help you?"

I was touched by his obvious sincerity. "I don't really think there is," I replied, "but I would really appreciate it if you would pray for me."

And then, not trusting myself to say any more without cracking up, I knelt down, expecting that he would lay his hands on my head. After kneeling with my eyes closed for several seconds, I was aware only of silence. I was temporarily disconcerted. Pastor Castellanos was not praying for me as I had asked. Instead, a few moments later, I felt his arms around me as he knelt down beside me. I was totally unprepared for what came next.

He started crying and in between his sobs he was asking God to heal my deepest wounds. I felt tears spurt out of my eyes, my defence mechanisms suddenly and totally demolished. I felt the love of Christ through the pastor in a way that I had seldom experienced. There is a passage in the Bible that says, "deep calls to deep", and there was something about the depth of this Colombian pastor's concern for a Christian brother he had never met before that unlocked the deep grief within me.

Pastor Castellanos held me so tight and continued to sob so deeply that, as I later remarked only half-jokingly, I thought I might have needed to comfort him. The reality was that by the time we said our goodbyes I felt lighter and cleaner, as if a whole build-up of anguish had been washed out of me. The kids too looked different, as if a load had lifted.

In those moments, when we had received such tender ministry in our time of need, I "got" what the church in Colombia was all about. It was not about systems or structures. Rather, I recognized that it was compassion for broken people that lay at the heart of the impact of this vast church in one of the most troubled countries in the world.

Maybe if we had not felt so broken ourselves, our visit to the church and its pastor would not have had the same big impact. But we were and it did.

Little did I know then how much all this would deepen my determination to reach out to people in need, nor could I have possibly envisaged at the time what was in store for future visits to Colombia.

One development that I did pick up on, however, was the increased concern that Wes was showing for the welfare of one particular member of our itinerant church group. At each session he seemed unusually willing to offer to Wilana such translation skills as he had developed during his days in Barcelona.

The fact that this personalized service required Wilana to move closer to Wes clearly appeared to both parties to be a very acceptable arrangement. This, however, was an arrangement that did not seem strictly necessary, given that Wilana, like the rest of the group, already had her own set of headphones tuned into the official conference translator.

Wilana, it later emerged, had already begun to see Wes in a new light. This stemmed from the night before we had left for Colombia, when Wes had gone round to her flat to see a mutual friend from LSE.

Wilana recalled: "That evening it struck me that Wes was a really nice guy. But I tried to put the idea out of my head because his brother was dating my sister and I knew that they would get married. I thought the idea of Wes and I getting together as well was too weird. Later that evening, before I fell asleep I read the words of Mark's gospel, which says, 'With man this is impossible, but not with God; all things are possible with God' [Mark 10:27].

"As I arrived in Bogotá I happened to be sitting next to him, and the first song was that all things are possible. Wes translated it. I thought this was really random."

At the time she kept her thoughts to herself, giving nothing away to her roommate, Melody. However, as they were now close friends they did have a heart-to-heart when Wilana asked Mel what kind of husband she thought would suit her. Mel went through a checklist. "You need someone who is a committed Christian, a leader, someone intelligent, someone who is fun, someone you can respect, good looking, sporty…"

Then she paused. Not previously having given credence to such a possibility, Mel now had an epiphany. "Oh, I'm describing Wesley!" At this point they both laughed at the apparent absurdity of the prospect. Wilana said nothing more on the subject. But Mel, without attaching much importance to it, did happen to note how often her brother's name seemed to be cropping up in Wilana's subsequent conversations.

Wilana's name was also at the forefront of a number of conversations I had with Wes. As we were sharing a room and jet lag was keeping us both awake, we had plenty of opportunity for late-night father/son chats. One of them sounded like a replay of a talk that James had had with me in South Africa:

"Dad, I really like Wilana. I don't know if she likes me. But I want to give it a go and ask her out. What do you think?"

"Wes, I think you should go for it," I said, reprising my earlier advice to James. "She's a great girl. You would do well."

Over the next few days I was confirmed in my opinion, as I had various opportunities over meals and in-between conference sessions to talk with Wilana. As she told me more of her background and gave her views on a wide range of subjects, I recalled Mel's checklist to Wilana of what she needed in a husband: "You need someone who is a committed Christian, a leader, someone intelligent, someone who is fun, someone you can respect, good looking, sporty…" I thought that all this equally applied to what Wes needed in a wife and that Wilana fitted the bill perfectly. I was intrigued to know how all this would play out.

As it happened, Maria Elia, the mutual Colombian friend from LSE, had invited both Wes and Wilana to stay on for a few days after the conference with her and her family in Barranquilla, one of Colombia's largest cities on the Caribbean coast and home of the pop singer Shakira.

Wes thought that this would provide the ideal surroundings to start dating Wilana. But he was not at all sure whether Wilana would see him as anything more than the future brother-in-law of her sister.

Just before the conference ended, Wes took his brother and sister into his confidence and told them of his intentions. Mel was protective towards her brother and tried to let him down gently. "I don't think she is going to say yes," said Mel, in a rare lapse from her usual insightful persona.

James was shocked when Wes told him of his bold intentions. James had originally thought, from witnessing their first meeting, that Wes and Wilana would one day get together. But mindful of how indifferent Wes had previously appeared towards Wilana, he was now taken aback by the abrupt change of opinion. He listened disbelievingly as his brother calmly detailed a proposed timeline for the unfolding of his romantic goals towards a girl who he wasn't even sure liked him:

"I am going to ask her out now in Colombia, get engaged at Easter in South Africa and go back there to marry her in December. That's the plan!"

All this amused me greatly. Wes, having first appeared to Wilana as a bookish Clark Kent figure, was now ready to fly at Superman speed in his wooing of her. I was very impressed with the faith and resolve of our first-born. It was refreshing to see Wes so happy and confident. I felt that he would not be disappointed.

After the healing time with Pastor Castellanos and mindful of what had already developed in South Africa between James and Vasti, I realized that I was finding it easier to dream again. The idea of a double blessing with two couples together did not strike me as fanciful, even if it was laughable.

My mind went back to a time shortly after Carol died when I had asked God to comfort our children. I had opened my Bible to Genesis 24:67 which tells how Isaac married Rebekah after the death of his mother Sarah. "So she became his wife, and he loved her; and Isaac was comforted after his mother's death."

At the same time a couple of other friends had independently come to see me to say that they felt that this verse had particular application to James. I did too.

But I had also prayed in my heart, "But what about Wes?" As I did, I had a very clear impression that Wes was also taken care of. "And Mel?" I also half-thought, half-prayed. At this point I remember just sensing a smile towards me. It was hard to fathom, but it felt more real than merely something I was imagining. Now, in Colombia, it was beginning to make more sense.

Wes decided he would make his move after the rest of us had left and before he and Wilana set out for the next part of their stay in Colombia. Mel, James and I were sworn to secrecy. We said our farewells at the last conference event in a big football stadium, with James risking a big wink at his brother when Wilana was not looking.

Then our protocol team got us safely to the airport. We boarded the plane for the long flight home, comforted by all that we had experienced and intrigued as we waited to know how Wilana would respond to the proposals that Wes was about to put to her.

Chapter 15
....

CHANGING THE GUARD

AFELY BACK IN ENGLAND, we took the call that we had been waiting for. James, Mel and I all wanted the phone. "So how did it go, Wes? Are you going out with Wilana?"

Wes kept us in suspense a little longer. He took his time to tell us what had happened after we had all left. He had picked his moment and said he would like a chat with Wilana. She had immediately assumed that he was going to clarify that their forthcoming visit to the Caribbean was nothing more than a pleasant trip by two good friends to see a mutual friend.

So she was caught off guard when Wes said that he had come to see her as more than a friend. "Actually, I like you a lot!" he said, borrowing a different line from *Dumb and Dumber* than the one James had used when asking Vasti out.

This had rendered Wilana speechless at first. Then, according to Wes, she "waffled on for ten minutes" and went through a list of pros and cons of why she might or might not be prepared to give her consent to a second Richards/Erasmus coupling.

Finally Wes, with an instinct that would help him in his future training as a lawyer, could not resist pressing for a verdict. "Is this a yes or a no?" he asked. At this point Wilana's less-than-overwhelming response was, "I can't see any reason why not."

Though not the most romantic of phrases, it had apparently been conclusive enough for them to seal the deal with a kiss or three. And so they told us that they had arrived safe and sound in northern Colombia where they were now having a great time.

What they did not tell us at the time, in fact not for some years, was that their journey had been interrupted when they had been stopped at an army checkpoint by young soldiers bearing shotguns who, after questioning them, had decided to let them continue on their way.

Wilana's only concern was how her younger brother might feel when he discovered that his two sisters were now going out with two brothers who had a single sister. She feared he might start to feel some pressure. She was right.

When she told him that she and Wes were now dating, Drikus, then just twenty, told her, "I can't believe it! Now everyone is going to expect me to get together with Mel."

Mel, as it happened, was not altogether elated about the latest developments either. She had really liked Drikus for some time, though she had been careful to give nothing away of her own feelings. Now she thought her brothers had really blown any chances of her getting together with Drikus. "Thanks a lot, boys!"

This seemed to be confirmed when Drikus had a chat with her. In as diplomatic a way as he could, he tried to convey the basic message that Mel should not get any ideas about any further close relationships developing between other members of the respective families. "Just because everyone else is getting together doesn't mean that we have to," he told her. Mel just laughed at such a nonsensical prospect.

I felt for Mel and sought to reassure my daughter by explaining that Drikus was only displaying classic symptoms that could easily be diagnosed as pure male panic. This seemed to amuse and satisfy Mel. She was content to put any romantic notions on hold for the time being. As it was, she had a big challenge to attend to.

A few months after her Mum's passing, she had come with me to a leaders' conference. I had spoken on how Joshua had stepped up into leadership following the death of Moses. At the end of the session Mel came to speak to me. "Dad, I think I need to step up and lead a women's conference like Mum used to. No one else will want to seem to be taking her place, so I feel I should keep things moving."

I was both touched and taken aback by this. I knew Mel would not suggest something like this just for sentimental reasons. But even though I was impressed by her courage, I still thought that this would be a big task for her. I suggested we talk with some of the senior leadership couples in the church. After listening to Mel give a clear account of all that she was feeling, they all agreed to support her. So too did Agu Irukwu, the senior pastor of a large Nigerian church in London, who was one of the guest speakers at the conference.

To Mel's great encouragement, he had sought her out for a chat. Knowing nothing of what Mel was considering, he said, "I have a very strong feeling that you are about to take on a responsibility that normally would be carried by a much older woman. Does this mean anything to you?"

So Mel set about organizing the conference, which she called "Standing in the Gap". Just as she was prepared to fill the empty space that had been left by her Mum, so she wanted women to see how they also should step out of their comfort zones to make a difference in the home, the church and the nation.

Her brothers and I were inspired to see the energy and commitment to excellence that Mel demonstrated as she led preparations for the conference. So too were the 500 women who turned up for the event.

There were poignant moments, especially for the family,

when delegates heard a recording of Carol speaking at what had proved to be her final women's conference. There were some tears too at the sight of eighteen-year-old Mel standing up to give her own keynote speech at the Windsor Parish Church, just by the spot where her mother's coffin had rested barely nine months before.

The memory is clear for many who were present. For at the very moment Mel began to talk, we heard music from outside. At first I wondered what it was. But then I realized that it was coming from a band of the Queen's soldiers. They were returning from the ceremony of Changing the Guard at Windsor Castle. It was a strong, if not prophetic, sign that we were now in a new phase of life, no matter how much we may have longed for a continuation of what had been.

The coming months were a time of rapid changes in the family. James took the opportunity of Vasti's visit to the women's conference to propose to her. He made sure they celebrated the occasion in some style. He arranged for them to be chauffeur-driven to various picturesque locations. At each one Vasti was given a gift. After a final stop at Windsor Castle they took a ride together in a horse and carriage on Windsor's Long Walk. Very romantic and very impressive, I thought.

Vasti evidently thought so too. She happily agreed to become James's wife and planned to move to the UK. This was a big move at any time for anyone used to the sun of South Africa but even more so as Vasti was the last Erasmus child to leave home.

Gert and Lina were to see more of the whole family, however, when all of us got together in Robertson at Easter, a few months after James, Mel and I had first travelled to South Africa. This time Wes was with us. He went for a walk with me and told me he was now ready to propose to Wilana. This he duly did at a friend's beach lodge on the Garden Route. Unfortunately they didn't see much of the beach or anything else, as there was a thick fog. But Wes was clear-sighted enough to seize the moment. He must have been confident of her response because he presented her with a ring from a London diamond dealer inscribed "South Africa". By this time Wilana had moved on from her line of "I can't see a reason why not" and readily agreed to his proposal.

With two weddings now on the horizon, some family discussion was called for. Would there be a double wedding or two separate weddings, and if so, who would get married when?

Both couples, not unreasonably, had their own ideas and dreams about their respective wedding days, so two weddings it would be. They all decided that James and Vasti should marry first, on 12 December, as they had been the first couple to get together. James and Vasti agreed that they would interrupt their honeymoon to return for the second wedding on 14 December.

Gert and I agreed that we would jointly conduct both weddings in English and Afrikaans. Meanwhile Lina, an expert dressmaker, would make the bridesmaids' dresses for both weddings. After such negotiations I wondered whether we should also be discussing dowries or maybe even gifts of cattle, but on reflection I thought that might be taking things too far. Gert, however, did not strike me as being totally convinced that this was such a crazy idea, when I mentioned it to him.

Mel was looking forward to being a double bridesmaid and Drikus was doing his best to look as calm and composed as he could under the circumstances. But increasingly, as I watched him and Mel interact together, I felt that it was only a matter of time before there would be a third union between the families.

They looked very much a couple and it was not long

before they were. Drikus remembers waking up one morning with a clear image in his mind of Mel. "Something suddenly switched in me. As I was making my coffee and thinking about Mel, I couldn't stop smiling. I called James and said, 'Listen, mate – I think I like your sister,' at which point James fell about laughing."

Given all the developing family connections and all that Mel had been through in relation to her Mum, I was pleased that Drikus came to talk to me about his feelings for Mel. I was impressed by his sincerity and character. In return, I tried to give him a Dad's perspective of my desire to see my daughter well treated, especially at a time of great vulnerability.

He left with my blessing and with no knowledge of how his dating proposal would be received. Although Drikus was by now fluent in his second language, English, Mel wondered why he was stumbling over his words when they went out on a walk together. When he did finally get to the point, Drikus said that Mel went mute before then agreeing to go out with him. They started dating on my fifty-third birthday.

This was a time of mixed emotion, as on that same day James was in hospital undergoing major reconstructive surgery after seriously damaging his knee in a soccer match.

This operation, though potentially very positive, was immediately very physically painful. Emotionally it was also hard for the family to handle as we found ourselves back in the whole routine of hospital. I did not find it at all easy being with James as I saw him slip under the anaesthetic, even though I knew the operation was routine and felt that all would be well.

James had a rough time initially but he had not lost his sense of humour. He had known of Drikus's interest in Mel. What he didn't know was that they had agreed to start dating on the same day as his operation. When James woke up in his room and saw Mel sitting on Drikus's lap, he assumed that the doctors had given him too much morphine.

With three kids from one family now improbably joined up with three kids from another family and James on the way to recovery, I marvelled at all that was developing so rapidly after such a dark period of life.

Even so, the first anniversary of Carol's death, two weeks after my birthday, brought many painful memories flooding back. For a week or two I was very subdued. Outwardly I had so much to be grateful for. Inwardly I was suddenly struggling again to feel motivated about anything.

I decided that grief was not unlike the board-game of snakes and ladders that we used to play as kids. Just when you think you are making progress up the ladder, you encounter a snake that sends you spiralling downwards.

For sure, I had received impressive and often unexpected deposits of God's grace over the previous twelve months. I had also found great strength through prayer and reading the Scriptures, particularly the Psalms and the second part of Isaiah, with its comforting vision of a new day. But from a practical point of view, I knew I needed to learn more of how to pace myself emotionally.

There were times, I discovered, when it was best not to think too much but just put your head down and work as hard as you could. I very much warmed to the approach of Sir Winston Churchill, whose motto in adversity was summarized as "KBO". The sanitized version of this is "Keep Battling On".

Mostly I thought that was the way to go, or too much life could be wasted in the present and the future by excessive preoccupation with the past. Yet there were other times when rest was best. Even that required balance. Sometimes it was helpful just to process things on my own, go for a walk and just take things quietly. At other moments it was life-enhancing just being able to relax in the company of loving family and friends. Keeping the discipline of a weekly day off and making the most of breaks proved to be very helpful emotionally, physically and spiritually.

A holiday later that summer certainly helped move me forward. Some friends in New York, Jonathan and Monica Lindsell, kindly offered me the use of their apartment with the excuse that they needed someone to look after their cat. Having had sudden visions of losing a favoured family pet among the skyscrapers, I was relieved to know that it was fine to bring with me responsible people like Mel and Terry and Margaret.

It was special to have quality father-and-daughter time in the company of friends who had been through everything with us. The weather too was something special, with sunny skies and ideal temperatures during our stay. One morning, as we left for a day of sightseeing, I remarked to the doorman, "What a beautiful day!" His instant response in a deep African American voice struck me profoundly: "Sir, every day is a beautiful day."

I reflected that African Americans, one way and another, had helped bring a lot of perspective and comfort to me in learning how to face up to trouble. I had long been inspired by the life and preaching of Dr Martin Luther King. I had been touched by various encounters with African American Christians, including the previous summer's meeting with Dr Charles Blake in Los Angeles.

I had also been shaped in my heart and worldview by a memorable month some years before, when I had lived in a large black church in a particularly dangerous area of Philadelphia as part of a team of pastors hosting a series of renewal and reconciliation services. The faith, fervour and fatherly love of the eighty-six-year-old senior pastor Ben Smith had made a hugely positive impression on me as I saw how he led a church of more than 5,000 people, so many of whom had known great pain in their lives.

Now, during our stay in New York, Mel was keen that we visited another largely African American church. She had been at a conference where one of the guest speakers was Dr A. R. Bernard, a former Black Muslim activist who was now senior pastor of the 25,000-member Christian Cultural Center in Brooklyn.

I was amused by the remarks of the very alert receptionist when we rang to find out details of the service. "Your accent tells me you are from England. I am sure our pastor would like to meet you after the service."

"How will we make contact with you in such a large crowd?" I innocently asked.

"Don't worry, we will find you," the receptionist said calmly.

When we arrived for the first service of the day I quickly realized that the task of locating us was not as problematic as I had imagined. The four of us were apparently the only white people present. We were instantly made to feel at home. The first song had barely been vibrantly sung before I was in tears. There was something that morning in the atmosphere and in the company of so many genuine African Americans, with their proven experiences of knowing God in times of trouble and emerging as overcomers, which brought a healing to my heart.

At the end of the service Pastor Bernard spent some time with us to speak further words of comfort to us. He prayed for us with an unforgettable compassion and sensitivity.

I thought about how much it had meant to me and to our family to have experienced the loving ministry of various pastors. I may have still wondered how it would happen, but I felt that

God would use the comfort that we had received to comfort others. I resolved afresh to keep going in ministry.

My friend Dr Mike Peters confirmed this when I spent some time back in St Louis, after Mel and Terry and Margaret had returned home. We were walking by a riverside when he suddenly turned to me and said: "Wes, you are going to make it!"

These seven simple, sincere words were a huge and timely boost to me. I was strengthened in my belief that not only would I make it, but so too would our family and church. Although the past was gone and the guard had changed, the future was, as my Dad used to say, "as bright as the promises of God".

At that moment two of the brightest prospects on the horizon for us were two marriages that would take place just before Christmas in the sunshine of South Africa.

Chapter 16

DOUBLE WEDDINGS

IGHTEEN MONTHS AFTER Carol's funeral, I was back in
South Africa for the third time. I was not alone. With
me were three children, three prospective children-in-
law and a sixty-strong British group who had come to celebrate
double weddings just before Christmas 2003.

It was fun watching the reactions of the first-time visitors
who were clearly as enthralled as we had been with the beautiful
vistas that greeted them. They were excited also to find that they
had "family" in Robertson, as Gert and Lina and their church
surpassed themselves in hospitality. Our group was hosted in
the homes and farms of church members. Whenever I contacted
any of them, they all seemed to be having endless outdoor *braais*.
They were all getting on with one another with an unexpected
ease, which helped to break down any lingering Afrikaner/
British divisions.

What was now becoming clear was that in addition to
the impending marriages, there was a strong union developing
between the two home churches of the kids. So to make the most
of our visit, we decided to hold a joint Christmas event where
all racial groups would be welcomed. The plan was that the
gifted singers and musicians in our party, plus the home-grown
talent in the church and children from the local community,
would provide the music and that, as part of the programme,

the three Robertson kids and the three English kids would tell their stories.

Word of this new development spread quickly, as in fact did most news in Robertson – sometimes, it seemed to me, even before it had happened. In the event and for the first time in the town, around 500 people – black, brown and white – joined together for a celebration of Christmas that often seemed more like a party than a service.

The couples enjoyed themselves too and seemed remarkably relaxed, given that the logistics of transcontinental weddings meant that there was still much to be organized. Vasti was so cool about everything that she only chose her tiara on the morning of her wedding. James, recognizing that he had met his match in the laid-back stakes, assigned Mel the responsibility of making sure that the bridesmaids' party operated by a clock and not a calendar.

For the weekend of the weddings I had rented an old Cape Dutch homestead so that the boys and I could have some time together. Despite all the joy and excitement, I knew it would not be easy for James, or any one of us who had known and loved Carol, when he stood up the next day to take his vows of lifelong commitment.

That became apparent when Wes, James and I were each moist-eyed as we prayed together a few hours before the first wedding. We had a big hug together. Even after that, in my room I shed more tears as I thought of how radiant and proud Carol would have been at the wedding. Once more I could vividly visualize her smile and hear her laughter. She would have had such fun.

It felt like total robbery that Carol, who had made her kids her main life's work, was not around to see her beloved boys marrying two very special girls whom she would have adored.

Yet thanks in such great part to her, James and Wes were now equipped to move into a new and happy season of their lives.

I found it hard to know how to handle the simultaneous feelings of intense joy and deep sadness, but finally I got the pent-up flood of emotion out of my system. I had a pray, looked out at more mountains that spoke of God's faithfulness, and got ready to conduct my son's wedding.

We arrived in good time and were soon joking around as we stood like stuffed penguins in our formal wedding suits with the sun beating down. Most of our fellow Brits were as overdressed as we were. Meanwhile the South Africans turned up smart, cool and casual.

The wedding venue, the Morgenhof Wine Estate, was somewhere Vasti had dreamed of when she was studying at nearby Stellenbosch University. This historic vineyard, situated on the slopes of the towering Simonsberg Mountains, dated back to 1692, just forty years after the founding of South Africa. Its cobbled courtyards and its old thatched white Cape Dutch hall gave a movie-like backdrop to the forthcoming union of a couple from two old countries.

As I stood awaiting the arrival of the bridal party, I surveyed the faces of so many friends, both old and new. I noticed that the long-time friends from home were also studying the faces of the boys and me. My thoughts, fortunately, did not drift too far, as the boys, standing smart and upright, were grinning as they considered whether or not they would have a lengthy wait for the bride.

I went out to check. There on time, thanks to Mel's best efforts, together with George and Terry in their conscripted roles as chauffeurs, stood a totally calm and smiling Vasti. She looked stunning in a dress and long train that she had designed herself.

I greeted Vasti, who was all smiles and exuding happiness. Gert looked distinguished and remarkably composed, given that he had spent the morning driving around on last-minute errands and was about to give his daughter away and then speak at the ceremony.

Mel was playing her part well but her smiles had a sadness about them. She did not trust herself to get through the reading of 1 Corinthians 13. At the last minute she asked Wilana to stand in for her. I gave her a quick hug, checked that everyone was ready to go, and took my place to start the service.

As a string-and-brass ensemble played, two young bridesmaids scattering petals led Vasti and Gert down the red-carpeted aisle. As she joined James for the start of the service, I had a privileged view of their smiling exchanges. I could read the pleasure and comfort in James's eyes and for a brief moment I had to gather myself.

Then, after I had welcomed friends and family from near and far, that little old building, which had remarkable acoustics, seemed to erupt in sound. The congregation powerfully and joyfully sang an old hymn beloved in both South Africa and Britain. It summed up well what we all felt: "To God be the glory, great things He has done…"

Simon, who had conducted the worship at Carol's funeral, now led the singing in English at a very contrasting service. Drikus took the lead for the Afrikaans version of the verses.

Vasti's enthusiastic singing was interrupted by her giggles as she took a sideways glance at James. He appeared to be reading the Afrikaans verses with great ease. His lips were somehow achieving a high level of synchronization with the words. This, I thought, was an impressive achievement, as neither he nor Wes had yet mastered much more Afrikaans than "*baie dankie*" ("thank you"), a limited although useful vocabulary, given that they were each acquiring a lovely South African wife.

In the event, the idea of James repeating his vows in Afrikaans was wisely abandoned. Gert explained that he would read out the formal vows in Afrikaans, after which James merely had to say "*Ja*" for "Yes". When the moment duly arrived, James's bold reply was: "*Ja, baie dankie!*" – thus linking all three Afrikaans words that he knew.

Like the rest of the congregation, I laughed at James's pleasure that he had so confidently conquered the briefest of sentences in Afrikaans. I also thought that he had demonstrated a touching trust that his future father-in-law had not inserted some extra clauses without his knowledge. If Gert had been asking him to fund annual holidays to the Bahamas for him and Lina, James would have been none the wiser.

When it came to the vows that James did understand, I could sense a tension in the congregation which I shared. I had noticed George wiping his eyes a few times and Wes did not look at ease. I had the driest throat that I had ever experienced in public speaking. I paused at the wrong place as I started to ask James whether he would take Vasti to be his wife.

James, however, quickly jumped into the gap with an eager "I will", drawing an instinctive response of "Not yet!" from me.

Though he told me later that he thought I had set him up for a joke, the unscripted repartee between father and son broke the tension, and from that point on everything was much more relaxed.

There was a tangible sense of family as we listened to the personal vows that James and Vasti had written for each other. Breaking the stereotype of an unexpressive British male, he told Vasti:

*When I see you, something happens within me that I
cannot rationalize or explain. I'm just moved. God,
the perfect planner, has brought your beauty into my
life. You are my best friend. Everything about you fills
me with a deep sense of love.*

*This love that grows between us is not just based
on passion or romance but it's based on a commitment
which grows with every passing day. My commitment
to you is born out of prayer and petition to heaven.*

James promised to "love and serve" Vasti "in both the big and
small things of life", and quoted Jeremiah 29:11, the text for the
title of this book. He then surprised us all with a closing flourish
in Afrikaans: "*Jy is baie mooi, ek het jou baie lief.*" ("You are very
beautiful, and I love you very much.")

Vasti, who I noticed swallowing hard, matched James in
demonstrating the power of sincerity in a world of cynicism.
She spoke of waiting all her life "for this moment" and of her
"joy and love and contentment that surpasses all understanding
because my heart has found its home. You have introduced me
to a new world of hopes, dreams and adventures. God's will for
my life has proved to be much higher than my own."

She spoke of the "tranquillity and inner peace" she
had found through the "tender love" of James, and of her
"honour, admiration and respect" for him. She promised to
"wholeheartedly encourage and support" him in every way.

As she came to her last lines and, mindful of all the big
changes of moving literally to a whole new world, away from
her parents, her friends and her sun-kissed home nation, Vasti
almost faltered. Her voice cracked as she quoted from the pledges
contained in the book of Ruth: "Where you go I will go, and
where you stay I will stay. Your people will be my people and

your God my God" (Ruth 1:16).

I took this verse (which had earlier formed part of my preaching series on "What becomes of the broken-hearted?") as the basis of my marriage talk. I pointed out that the promises that James and Vasti had just made were "considered, deep and based on a biblical teaching of covenant which means an agreement of unshakeable and unbreakable loyalty".

Such lifelong faithfulness is becoming less common today. People trade in a husband or wife today as you might trade in a car. But marriage is not a disposable commodity. It is intended to go the whole distance.

Covenant love is the basis of real marriage. Such committed love between husband and wife is not just about feelings, emotions or outward beauty. It is an agreement to be faithful and true in every situation and circumstance, "as long as you both shall live".

I stated my belief that, just like Ruth and Naomi, James and Vasti would not only know great comfort from such commitment, but also discover that their covenant relationship would have great consequences for their own blessings and the blessings of many people.

James and Vasti were taking it all in but James was also clearly mindful that in keeping with local tradition, he and his bride were standing throughout the whole service. He shot me a pleading look of the variety that used to melt his Mum, as if to say: "Thanks for the sermon, Dad, but keep it short."

So I kept my talk mercifully brief. After some prayers and more songs, James and Vasti buoyantly left the flower-bedecked wedding chapel to a song Vasti had chosen. Inevitably, perhaps, it was "Son of a Preacher Man".

As sons – and daughters – of preacher men, and preacher men themselves, got together for photographs, James told me he couldn't help thinking about who else should have been posing alongside us amid the breathtaking scenery. In his wedding speech, under the chandeliers of the cosy old wine cellar, he paid special honour to his Mum and Dad and brother and sister.

Mostly, however, despite some sadness, there was an air of great fun and festivity as English and Afrikaners enjoyed a great dinner, music and dancing. James and Vasti led the way in this, taking the floor to the strains of Etta James's "At Last!"

After a long evening and goodbye hugs to the family, James and Vasti were whisked away to their honeymoon suite by the ocean in Cape Town.

I felt very satisfied, if still a little emotional, after a wonderful day. But any lingering sentiment of mine at the departure of the newlyweds was tempered by the knowledge that they were due to come back in less than thirty-six hours. This time roles would be reversed with James and Vasti as best man and bridesmaid, and Wes and Wilana as bride and groom.

When James and Vasti reappeared they received a number of predictable enquiries of mock concern from friends as to whether they had got enough sleep in the time since we had last seen them.

The second part of the wedding double act took place just outside Stellenbosch in the cinematic surrounds of the Zorgvleit wine estate. The backdrop of vineyards, horses in green pastures and rugged mountains was truly dramatic. Whereas wedding number one was like being on a film set, wedding number two felt like we were filming on location.

Guests were ferried through the rolling acres in ancient Dutch carts to a wedding chapel with a more recent history than James's and Vasti's venue. The finishing touches had been applied only that morning, and Wes and Wilana were to be the first of a long line of couples to be married in what has since become a major wedding venue.

Standing around in the spacious grounds and chatting with the boys and the guests who were now getting a decided taste for all things South African, was a much more relaxed experience after all the emotions of the first wedding.

Everyone had enjoyed a day off to unwind. Wes and I had a memorable father/son dinner at an outstanding restaurant in Franschhoek where we reviewed so many experiences that we had shared and affirmed our love and appreciation for each other. As we came to the end of our meal a violinist appeared at our table, stood next to Wes and played the Alan Jay Lerner song, "I'm getting married in the morning".

Wilana and the girls were not having such a relaxed time the next morning as hairdressers, dress-fitters and make-up artists came and went. When the bridal party appeared, Wilana, the tallest of the Erasmus children, looked every inch the fashion model in her exquisitely fitted wedding dress and with her hair swept up. The bridesmaids, including Vasti and Mel reprising her role from forty-eight hours before, all looked like something out of a glamour magazine in their blue satin dresses.

As Wilana came down the aisle with Gert, she exchanged smiles with Wes. I had a freeze-frame moment with the couple in love in the foreground and blue skies and mountains beyond the open chapel doors in the background.

I felt almost overwhelmed by God's faithfulness. I could see that something similar was happening with Wes and Wilana as the congregation sang out the first hymn.

It quickly dawned on me that this wedding too would be more emotional than I had anticipated. Once more the vows came early in the service and once again there came an unusual silence.

This time there were no false starts from me, but when it came to Wes repeating the lines, "in sickness and in health… till death us do part", he paused and then stopped. He just couldn't say the words.

I looked up to see tears in his eyes. Our family were also tearful; so too were most of the congregation, including some big Afrikaner guys.

I reached out to console Wes, just about managing to hold it together myself. Wilana, quickly realizing that we all needed a bit of steadying, leaned across and gently brushed her bridegroom's cheek.

After some moments, Wes managed to complete his pledge of lifelong allegiance. Then, with some feeling, he delivered his personal vows.

When he finished Wilana smiled and then left his side. Momentarily he looked confused, until his bride sat down at a nearby piano, looked her bridegroom in the eyes and expressed her vows in a song she had written specially for him. She sang with such feeling that Wes looked as if he were in a wonderful dream – which in truth he was, after a long nightmare.

My own talk began with an acknowledgment that "this wedding is proof that God does indeed hand out double blessings. Twice in one weekend I have the great privilege of jointly conducting the marriage of a much-loved son and a very special daughter-in-law."

Of course, I could not resist reminding Wes that the wedding was also evidence of how radically he had revised his earlier comment to the family that "Wilana is your friend, not mine!"

I said that his Mum would both have approved of Wilana and been amused by the romantic effect that she had had on her son. For myself, I said I believed that they were "ideally suited to each other in personality, character, faith, dreams and even height".

My wedding verse for Wes and Wilana was Psalm 103:17–18. I spoke of how they were each recipients of the Lord's great mercy and blessings that had been experienced throughout generations of each of their families. They now had been entrusted with a covenantal responsibility to keep God at the centre of their lives and to stand out and stand up for truth and righteousness.

As they had been literally standing for some while, I did not prolong my talk, and Wes and Wilana were soon making a joyous exit into the brilliant sunshine and to an African band that had everybody swaying.

That evening was like an invitation to a biblical banquet of so many good things, the greatest of which was love: not only love between the new couple and the love of an extended family and friends, but also the very love of God that had kissed this whole happy weekend.

As Wes and Wilana started their honeymoon and James and Vasti resumed theirs, I knew that I was a very rich man.

Chapter 17

COMPLETING THE WEDDING TRILOGY

A YEAR LATER ALL THE EXTENDED new family got together for a more relaxed Christmas break in Cape Town. But another wedding was very much on Mel's mind as I rode the cable car with her to the top of Table Mountain. She pointed down to the beautiful contours of Camps Bay, with its turquoise waters and shimmering sandy beaches, and declared, "That's where I want to get married!"

Fortunately for Mel, though unknown to her at that moment, Drikus had similar ideas. He had been to see me for a talk about their future just before we had left home. The discussion had seemed to cover a wide range of generalized subjects until Drikus finally came to the point. "Uncle Wes…" he began, using the traditional Afrikaner term of respect for an older man; then, adopting a traditional English phrase for such occasions, he formally asked, "… can I have your daughter's hand in marriage?"

I'm afraid I couldn't resist responding with, "Is that all you want?"

"Uncle Wes, give me a break! This is tough enough as it is!"

At this point I fancied that Carol would have told me to go easy on him, something that Drikus seemed to appreciate when I shared my thoughts with him. I told him how delighted she would have been that her daughter would marry such a great guy and that she had approved of him on the first and only occasion that they had met.

I said that I too was happy that he would become my son-in-law as well as the husband of my daughter, not to mention the brother-in-law of his sisters' husbands. By now I had to think twice about the various permutations of relationships.

Like Wes and James before him, he too made a pilgrimage to my jeweller contact in Hatton Garden and selected a classy ring for Mel, which I knew she would love. Now, on a sunny December morning, at the top of Table Mountain, Drikus tried to subtly draw Mel away from the family group so that he could present the ring to her. Thinking he had found a solitary spot, he bent down uncomfortably on one knee to propose. Mel's initial surprise quickly gave way to instant acceptance. The moment was sealed with a kiss and unexpected applause from previously unnoticed tourists who had witnessed the whole scene.

The rest of the families were not far away and when we all got together we could only laugh and shake our heads in disbelief that the unlikely wedding trilogy between the three kids from one family and three kids from another was actually going to happen.

Not surprisingly, as father of the bride, I felt a big responsibility about this wedding. I resolved to do all I could to make it as memorable as possible. I felt it keenly that our only daughter did not have her Mum with her to share in all the joy and excitement.

I also knew just how clueless I was about wedding preparations. Wedding ceremonies were no problem to me; I had conducted plenty. But just the prospect of getting a grip on the details of wedding planning and wedding dresses made me want to lie down. I did not know one end of a train from another.

So I decided to treat the whole thing as a shared venture of discovery for Mel and myself. As it turned out, we had a lot of fun. Mostly it was at my expense – in every sense of the word.

We canvassed family and friends for their ideas and spent many hours doing our own research and planning. We were put in contact with a first-rate wedding planner, Carla, who quickly became enamoured with the whole family story and worked with us more like a big sister to Mel than as a business advisor. Since the legal ceremony would take place in England, we could be as creative as we wanted to be with the South African wedding event.

Mel and Drikus had decided they would marry on 15 December 2005, the day before his twenty-third birthday and just after the wedding anniversary dates of James and Vasti (12 December) and Wes and Wilana (14 December). The logistics of the unusual family combinations, we were discovering, required a lot of planning.

For this wedding the family roles would change, with James as best man and Wilana and Vasti as bridesmaids. Wes would assist Gert with conducting the wedding, and I would join them in their duties after I had given Mel away.

Three months before the wedding, Mel and I went to South Africa on a pre-marriage planning trip and toured more wedding shops than I ever imagined existed. As for venues, we were spoilt for choice in the Western Cape. In the end we decided to hang convention. So we went for three of them.

We hit on the idea of having a wedding worship service at a local church in Camps Bay. Then we would move along the coast road to the Twelve Apostles Hotel for the actual vows and marriage ceremony. Finally we would have a reception in the

Rotunda of the Bay Hotel just across from the beach, which would be ideal for photographs.

As the implications of organizing what amounted to three separate events and attendant transport issues began to sink in, I took a daily interest in the exchange rates, which fortunately were favourable. I was very grateful for the local prices which made our plans possible.

For all the undoubted and appreciated temporal blessings we were experiencing, there was still an underlying sadness that would sometimes surface unexpectedly as Mel and I went about our preparations. One morning I took her for a breakfast treat at the famous old colonial Mount Nelson Hotel. We were served by one of the older black waitresses, Margaret Roberts, who seemed to have time to chat to all the customers. She was clearly regarded with some veneration by regular visitors.

She chatted to us and drew out why we were together in South Africa. She then told us how she had been widowed over ten years previously and how tough her life had often been. Then, not knowing anything of our own Christian experience, she smiled at us with a tender and knowing look and told us with great simplicity and sincerity of someone she knew who could help us through good times and bad times.

"I have discovered how Jesus has always been there for me, and He's there for you too. He will never fail you and He will never leave you. All you have to do is open your heart to Him and He will heal your heart and help you through everything."

I looked at Mel and could see that she was as affected as I was by this seemingly random conversation with a stranger who had taken such an interest in us. I thanked Margaret and she smiled as we filled her in on our background. I told her, "You do not know how much your words mean to us right now."

We left the hotel with a lightness of spirit that was hard

to describe. For me, this was just one more example of God as a Good Shepherd, reminding us that not only was He with us "through the valley of the shadow of death", but that also He was leading us into "green pastures".

By the time the wedding came around I felt a great sense of gratitude for what we were about to enjoy. I was thankful too not only for God's faithfulness but also for the tremendous support of friends and fellow leaders who had stuck with us through all the trials and transitions. Scores of them were now with us again and others who didn't make the first weddings had travelled for this one.

Our friends, J.P. and Shane Rangaswami, had hired a big house facing the ocean in Camps Bay. As Mel clearly could not get married from her UK home, they very generously invited all our family to share their holiday home, which would double up as Mel's wedding base.

It was here, early on the morning of the wedding, that Mel and I met up for a chat before all the events of the day got under way. We stood on a balcony that had panoramic views of the coastline and Table Mountain. We reflected once more on the now-familiar words of Psalm 121 and how God had brought us to this day of favour.

We reminisced about Carol. I told Mel what a total joy she had always been to her Mum and me and her brothers, and gave her a big hug.

And then we set out to make the most of her big day. For all the comings and goings of Carla's wedding team, there was a remarkable absence of any stress and the sun shone in from every angle.

I was pleased with how composed I was until Mel, more beautiful than I had ever seen her, stood before me in her wedding dress. Then I nearly lost it. Thankfully, for both of us, I quickly got a grip and we had an easy chat on the way to the church.

Just before we arrived, a recording of one of Mel's favourite Christian songs, Michael W. Smith's "Healing Rain", had been played to the congregation. By the time we got to the church it seemed like some of that healing rain had already fallen. There was a very special atmosphere of peace and joy as I accompanied Mel down the aisle to Wagner's "The Bridal Chorus" from *Lohengrin*.

There were lots of smiles coming our way but there were tears too in quite a few eyes. My old friend Ken Gott, who had done so much to help us through our initial bereavement, was struggling to establish eye contact with me.

Drikus's face was a picture of delight as he saw Mel. I noticed Wes, who was standing to greet the wedding couple, taking in the conflicting emotions of the moment. I was glad that he was conducting this part of the ceremony.

He did very well to put us all at ease. Simon Goodison, in town again and back on wedding duty, led us in the by-now-familiar combination of worship in English with some assistance with the Afrikaans.

Drikus and Mel had wanted this first service to be a time of joint dedication of their lives to God, and to focus on God's love and greatness through Bible readings, prayers, powerful contemporary worship songs and great old hymns. Their choices said much about their convictions and experiences: "Majesty", "King of Kings", "The Steadfast Love of the Lord Never Ceases", "Here is Love Vast as the Ocean", "Shout to the Lord" and "How Great Thou Art". The Raymond Badham song "Magnificent" was particularly poignant with its lines about the Lord "who calmed the raging seas that came crashing over me".

I needed some of that calmness as I stepped up to preach

at my daughter's wedding, I felt both privileged to be asked and daunted by the emotional challenge. I felt as if I was speaking in a glass case, but Mel and Drikus appreciated what I said and it was well received.

Gert did a great job with his speech and this first service ended with a wonderful lightness of spirit. Mel and Drikus did not exactly formally walk back down the aisle. They seemed to bounce out to the Dixie Cups song, "The Chapel of Love".

By the time we managed to recover our breath and catch up with them outside, they were upstairs on one of the double-decker London-style open-topped buses which we had hired and onto which older and younger had clambered with the enthusiasm of young kids. Everyone was given bottles of water to help them cope with the heat. The trip along the winding coastal road looked like a scene from a 1960s Cliff Richard movie. Certainly it was a testimony to the happiness of innocent fun.

Our destination, the Twelve Apostles, was not chosen for religious reasons, although I thought it amusingly appropriate in view of our convictions on developing disciples of Christ. Rather, we picked it because it had the most amazing views, with Table Mountain at the back and the Atlantic Ocean at the front.

The other major benefit of switching locations for the second part of the service was that I was able to walk Mel down the aisle for the second time in one day. This time the red-carpet walk was longer. We were all more relaxed and I savoured every moment of walking with, talking to and looking at Mel before giving her away to be the wife of Mr Johannes Hendrikus Erasmus.

When the time came for Gert to enquire, "Who gives this woman to be married to this man?", I thought I said my lines particularly well. I had been practising my "I do."

Then I switched places to face the bride and groom and lead them through their formal vows. This they managed to do without any of the hitches experienced at the weddings of their brothers and sisters.

Their own vows came next and clearly touched everyone who heard them, as I was well positioned to notice. Facing Drikus, Mel told him that she could:

> *hardly believe I am standing before you now as your wife. I could not have foreseen the events that followed after I met you in Windsor four years ago. And now, here we are, in the most beautiful place in the world, in Africa with so many of our close friends and family.*
>
> *I'm confident that we are a match made in heaven. I know you love me because I see it in your eyes, I hear it in your voice, and I feel it in your touch. I feel safe in your arms and safe in the knowledge that I am to spend the rest of my life with you.*
>
> *Although these past few years have been the worst in my life, you have also made them the very best. You brought so much joy, peace and happiness into my life. You taught me how to laugh again and be myself. You loved me in spite of my sadness. You loved me because of my sadness. You have wiped away many tears from my face and you have stayed close to me many times in my sadness. You wanted to see me happy, to see me smile, to see me enjoy life again. Thank you for helping me to do that. You are my best friend.*

Mel spoke also of Drikus's faith and hunger for God.

> *You dream the biggest and the best for you, me, our family, our future family and many others less fortunate than us.*

> *You worship the Lord with all your heart, and*
> *it was that gentleness of your spirit and the passion*
> *in your eyes as you played music and sang to the Lord*
> *which made me fall in love with you.*

And with that Mel pledged her "wholehearted and unreserved love" to Drikus, "for now and always."

Drikus looked appropriately affected by these words and then responded eloquently with some of his own:

> *Simply being in your presence and looking into your*
> *eyes makes me appreciate life and all that God's*
> *gracious hand has given to me. You always make me*
> *smile and always help me to see the precious things in*
> *life.*
>
> *To me you are a true English rose. From the*
> *first moment I recognized your beauty, I increasingly*
> *discovered the immeasurable treasure I had in you.*
> *It has been my honour and privilege to support and*
> *comfort you in any way in the past and I commit to*
> *doing so in the future.*
>
> *Equally, you have been such a support and*
> *inspiration to me. To me you are the very example of*
> *what a true Christian, best friend and wife should be.*

He too quoted from Jeremiah 29:11, that "God's plan for us is to prosper us and not to harm us, to give us hope and a future."

As he concluded his vows, Drikus smiled at his bride and then left her side for a moment. He picked up one of his guitars and then proceeded to serenade Mel with a ballad he had composed earlier on the wedding morning.

The quality of his singing and the creativity of his words

had nearby hotel residents listening in. As for Mel, I will never forget her look of contented contemplation as she listened to her new husband pledge his love to her in heartfelt verses and a refrain that said:

Never did I know a love this much
The deepest part of my heart you touch
And I can't believe this day has come
And I am so sure that you're the one
I want to go with you wherever He will lead us
from here on.[15]

And so, with the deepest part of pretty much everyone's heart touched, Drikus rejoined his smiling wife and led her out to a sun-kissed garden and into a new beginning.

That evening, after I gave my father-of-the-bride speech and as Mel's beloved chocolate fountain overflowed at a fairytale wedding reception, I slipped outside to a wooden viewing deck for some time alone. I looked up to Table Mountain which towered above and which was perfectly illuminated by the moon.

As the warm night breezes blew across me, I wished Carol was by my side to share this moment. And though she was not there, I thought of how much she had done to shape her three kids who were now all happily married to three other great kids from another family.

I slowly shook my head, at first in sadness and then in amazement at all that had happened since the loss of my own unforgettable bride. Then I went back inside to rejoin the party and dance with our girl, the new Mrs Erasmus.

---

15 Copyright © Johannes Hendrikus Erasmus.

Chapter 18

....

TWO BABIES AND A PRESIDENT

ITH THREE CHILDREN now married, I pondered what the future might hold. Early in the autumn of 2006 I got a clue when James and Vasti popped in to see me for a chat. I was not prepared for what they had to share. "Dad, you are going to be a grandad!" said James, smiling.

For a moment I didn't know what to say. "Did he say *grandad*?" I thought to myself, quickly recognizing that this was another of those big happy/sad moments that can strike without warning when you so want to share good news with someone who is no longer around.

Then, as the good news dawned on me, I congratulated the prospective Dad and Mum and joked that I felt too young to be a grandfather – a classic case of self-delusion. In all the back and forth, I managed to establish that the new arrival was due early the following May.

A few days later, when I was in South Africa with Gert and Lina, they called me to say that Wes and Wilana were now appearing on their computer screen and that our respective firstborns wanted a word with us all. "Hi, everyone, we just wanted to let you know that we are having a baby too!"

"When?" we all asked at the same time. "Early next May," they replied, clearly amused to see the disbelieving and delighted reactions of the parents.

Maybe I should have expected this. The boys had a long track record of parallel achievements, all the way from their school days and rowing days to marrying two sisters. But, seriously, what were the chances of this?

And so, within seventy-five hours in early May 2007, two baby boys entered our family. Samuel Wesley Johannes was born, nine days early, to Wesley and Wilana. Joseph James Isaiah then made his appearance to James and Vasti in the same room that his cousin had just vacated.

One nurse who had left the maternity unit after helping with Wilana's delivery came back on duty to find someone who looked very much like Wilana about to have a baby. It took a little while to explain the story to her and even then she did not look entirely sure about what was going on.

Even for us, it took a while for the latest developments in the family story to sink in. The joy of this new day really hit me when the boys were brought home and a grandson was placed in each of my arms.

I looked up to see what an emotional moment this was for all the family. I sighed, smiled and shed a few tears all at the same time. Then, as I looked down at these two tiny sleeping figures, I gave thanks to God for them and spoke some blessings from the Bible over them.

Not long afterwards, as Gert and Lina were still visiting us, we held a very happy public dedication service for the new arrivals with all the church.

The practical realities of having grandchildren were soon obvious, as the couples asked if I would like to take my turn in changing nappies. It amused me to see how willing they were to share some of their parental responsibilities with me. I told them that of course I would be delighted to do so in emergencies, but purely in the interests of their own development as parents I thought it best that they should attend to these essential duties themselves.

As I watched their early and, for the most part, impressive efforts, I told them how privileged they were to be able to use easy stick-on nappies, or whatever they were called. When our kids were babies their Mum and I had to use great skill not to impale them with safety pins.

Mel, however, revelling in her new role as an aunt, was always quick to volunteer as a stand-in nappy changer, while the brave Drikus, who had camped outdoors in Africa, demonstrated a physical reaction to such a role, quickly distancing himself from any action. I found this an entertaining spectacle and looked forward to the day when he too would become a Dad. "I'll be all right when the time comes," Drikus reassured me, adding quickly, "but it hasn't come yet!"

It didn't seem long before Gert and Lina were once more reunited with their grandsons at Christmas. The babies were already bonding and having crawling races in their matching seasonally red outfits. Both of them were big smilers and had cheeky grins. No surprises there.

Moreover, they were both sleeping well, a great grace to James particularly, as he woke up three or four times a night for the first three years of his life. Mostly it was me who used to get up for him. Carol had developed a considerable expertise in kidding me that she was in a deep sleep, if not a coma.

James would always greet my arrival with a sweet smile and readiness to play games. Despite the almost permanent feelings of jet lag, I actually had a lot of fun spending time with the little high-energy guy.

Now, a generation later, I loved hanging out with my grandsons. That Christmas, with these new little characters in our lives, I considered how far we had been able to move forward since the last Christmas before Carol died and our first Christmas without her.

She was in many ways still a big part of our lives and seldom out of our thoughts, especially at family events. Yet she would have been so thrilled to know that we had come to a new kind of peace.

So much had happened in our lives that Carol had not shared in. Our daughters-in-law whom she had never met now regularly made themselves at home in her kitchen. Her son-in-law was now living with his wife Mel in our home.

Mel and Drikus had graduated together from Royal Holloway University of London, following in the footsteps of Wes and James. Drikus went into marketing with a multinational IT company. Mel was to work for the Centre for Social Justice in Westminster after completing her Master's degree at the London School of Economics.

Wes, meanwhile, had returned to further education to study law. Later on we had some more moving moments when Wes was called to the Bar at the Middle Temple in London. Carol had passed this distinguished location many times on her way to treatment at Barts, not knowing that one day her son, dressed in wig and gown, would be celebrating her memory there.

Wes was now, however, not pursuing law but working part time for the Chairman of Alpha International at London's Holy Trinity Brompton and part time at his home church.

James was head of operations at our home church. All three couples were closely involved in the church's ministry and leadership team, a family involvement that had been birthed when they all spoke at Carol's funeral.

As for me, I felt far more settled in myself. I had long since cleared the wardrobe of Carol's stuff and renovated most of our home. It had felt particularly strange having a new kitchen installed, as the old one had been so much Carol's domain. Yet all these changes were a necessary part of moving into a new season of family life.

My focus was now far more on the future than the past. I had often thought of the advice of a wise preacher who said: "Be careful to look where you are going because you will go where you are looking. If you look back you will go backwards. If you look forward you will go forward."

Increasingly I found myself focusing on how to reach out to people at home and abroad who did not know of the love of God. I wanted our church and all churches to minister more effectively to so many people who, like ourselves, had experienced brokenness in their lives and who needed the reality of Christian hope.

I particularly concentrated my time and effort on training leaders in our home church and in South Africa and Sri Lanka, where we had also developed links. I felt privileged to serve with so many high-quality, committed people who were united in common purpose across the continents.

I was moved by the warmth and vitality of the Sri Lankan Christians, led by Pastors Roshan and Liz Wickramasinghe, even as they faced up to threats of persecution for their faith, sometimes in conditions of considerable poverty. Their level of commitment was inspiring. So too was the atmosphere when they fervently sang their praises to God – an experience, I thought, that would touch the hardest heart.

As for South Africa, our bond grew with every visit and spoke volumes of the reconciliation that comes through common faith in Christ. Not only were brown, white and black people now joining together in common community, but we Brits were warmly received by many Afrikaners.

This in itself represented major progress. Even on our

Two Babies and a President

early visits we had not realized just how deep were some of the wounds left by the Boer War, generations after one of the most bitter conflicts in history. We met Afrikaners who opened up to us and told us how a legacy of bitterness had affected their lives and their attitudes towards the English.

At one of our ministry weekends in Robertson I had said how sorry I was, as an Englishman, to learn about the suffering inflicted by my countrymen that had led to the deaths of 15 per cent of the Afrikaner population, mostly women and children. I asked if all of those who still felt affected by this, could find it in their hearts to forgive. One older lady told me the next day that she had done this and that she had slept soundly for the first time in many years.

Time and again I discovered how our own journey of sadness and healing somehow connected us to people and nations who had also known pain of one sort or another. Our own experiences had undoubtedly given us a new awareness of human need, but also we were attracted to those who were motivated and able to minister effectively to people in need. This was particularly true of our links with Colombia. Our continuing friendship with Pastors César and Claudia Castellanos helped us greatly and also led to many further unexpected developments.

Before Carol died, going to Colombia had never been in my plans. Even on our memorable first visit I had no idea of what would unfold on a further trip five years later.

In late January 2008, however, I was back in Colombia with Wes and Wilana, James and Vasti and the two grandsons. On our arrival our guide casually mentioned that I would be a keynote speaker the following morning at the 18,000-seat coliseum, which was news to me. This plan, that had clearly lost something somewhere in translation, persuaded me to go straight to my hotel room and stay there for some prayer and preparation.

I knew what I should say, even though I had expected to share the main points as part of a brief greeting. However, despite the scale of the occasion, tiredness got the better of me. I decided that the best plan would be to rest and trust God for tomorrow's "daily bread".

I was almost asleep when I heard a phone ring. It was our guide calling to give me an update on the next day's proceedings, which had only just been confirmed, presumably for security reasons. "The President of Colombia will be attending in the afternoon," she said. "Would you address him on behalf of the international delegates?"

My thoughts were not exactly moving at warp speed, but even so, I registered that this was a significant invitation. I managed to say that I would be very happy to speak and I put the phone down. A few moments later my befuddled state rapidly cleared as it dawned on me that tomorrow would be a far bigger day than I had anticipated.

I phoned the boys in their rooms and told them of the imminent privilege and responsibility facing their Dad. They, like me, were struck by the thought of how radically circumstances had changed since Pastor Castellanos had first prayed for one very hurting family.

I put them on alert to help me with research and then decided once more that rest at this point was the best option in readiness for the next day. I arranged for an early morning call and, thankfully, fell quickly into a deep sleep.

The next morning I was up by 5 a.m. for the start of a memorable day. By the time we reached the coliseum it was packed. As I stood backstage waiting to be called to the platform, I read my neatly typed notes and then needlessly reread them. But I did not feel entirely at ease.

I felt like young David in King Saul's ill-fitting armour. So

I decided to leave my notes behind and just refer to my little travel Bible with a few scribbled bullet points. I had prepared as well as I could. I knew what I wanted to say. Now I needed to anticipate what the famous Welsh preacher Dr Martyn Lloyd-Jones called "the romance" of preaching.

By that he meant that you only discovered what God would do in the hearts and minds and wills of people when you were actually preaching. "What one had never thought of, or even imagined, suddenly happens in the pulpit while one is actually preaching, and one is left with a sense of amazement, gratitude and unspeakable joy. There is nothing like it,"[16] the good doctor had written. "You never know who is going to be listening to you, and you never know what is going to happen to those who are listening to you."[17]

That was exactly my experience that morning in Bogotá as I faced the biggest congregation that I had yet preached to. I began by sharing the story of how Wes and Wilana had greeted each other at a previous conference, just as many delegates had done moments before. I joked that you never knew where such greetings could lead and told how Wes and Wilana had got married later that year.

I told them how, that same weekend, Wes's brother and Wilana's sister had also got married and how, two years later, the sister of the brothers and the brother of the sisters had followed suit. This unlikely story drew a big and enthusiastic response from the Latin American crowd and the international delegates.

And then they listened intently when I told them of the sadness that had preceded the joy and of how reluctant I had been to come to Bogotá that first time. I said how I had felt the

---

16   D. Martyn Lloyd-Jones, *Preaching and Preachers*, London: Hodder & Stoughton, 1971, p. 299.
17   Lloyd-Jones, *Preaching and Preachers*, p. 301.

love of God in a very deep way when Pastor Castellanos had wept with us. "That was the start of a great healing in my life. But in those moments I also felt a great love for multitudes of people who are so broken and in need of great healing."

I took as my text Jonah 4:11 where God asks His angry prophet a penetrating question: "Should I not be concerned about that great city?" Jonah wanted the godless and bloodthirsty Ninevites wiped out. God wanted them saved. I said that God's heart is for people and that we too must have God's heart for men and women everywhere.

> *Sometimes God has a hard job of convincing those of us inside the church, especially His leaders, of how much love He has for those outside the church.*
>
> *God loves people despite the wrong they have done, and so must we. God does not delight in the death of the wicked. It is not His will that anyone should perish. God wants all to be saved and to come to the knowledge of the truth.*
>
> *God cares for people who neither know Him nor care about Him. God's compassion here in the book of Jonah extends even to domestic animals. God is concerned about all His creation and about what matters to people.*

As the sermon progressed I could see that the people were being considerably moved by these truths. I was too. When the preaching was finished there were many tears as thousands of Christians prayed fervently together.

As soon as I was off stage, I had some moments alone to absorb what had just happened and to marvel that God had made such a thing possible in my life.

A few hours later, after a lunchtime break of rapid speech-writing, my sense of wonder at unforeseen developments increased when I was back on stage again waiting to be introduced to the President of Colombia, Álvaro Uribe.

The coliseum was filled once again with people. Everyone was in position early as the building, with a strong army presence inside and outside, had been locked down for security reasons. A smell of petrol just offstage alerted me to the President's arrival as his convoy parked inside the building.

The next moment we were all standing to attention as the crowd enthusiastically greeted the arrival of a political leader with unprecedented popularity ratings in his own nation.

I was briefly introduced to him and was immediately struck by how relaxed this slim, bespectacled man was, given that he lived under constant threat of assassination and that his own father had been killed by FARC terrorists. His manner was one of calm authority and personal warmth.

My proximity to him focused my thoughts about how vulnerable any person is, no matter how powerful, and that all our lives and times are in God's hands. The big issue, it seemed to me, was being ready to meet God at any moment.

This thought helped me to feel unusually relaxed. I was glad that the army and the sniffer dogs had done a thorough job; at least I hoped they had. But overall I figured that as the Lord had brought us through so much, then I should trust Him now.

I had seen how Carol had trusted God in life and death and I had seen how God had presided over all our comings and goings as a family. Now as I listened to the enthusiastic singing of the Colombian national anthem, I looked from the platform to the concrete seats on my left where I had sat so disconsolately on my first visit.

I looked out at the crowd and saw my two sons and their

wives smiling at me and holding up my two grandsons. At that moment I was stunned. I was grateful beyond words to realize how far God had brought us in our journey to date.

And then, anthem over, my focus switched as I was called to speak directly to the leader of a nation who had been through many trials of his own and who had presided over many positive and obvious changes in his nation. I had witnessed many of these on the occasions I had visited.

In my speech I noted that much of the "remarkable and continuing turnaround in Colombia's turbulent story" was due to President Uribe's visionary, resolute and courageous leadership, something that Western politicians "should not forget". I also thanked him "for having also the wisdom and humility to appreciate the influence of Christianity in the transformation of a nation."

I continued, "A nation is favoured when there is great internal change in the hearts of individuals and families through great numbers committing their lives to Jesus Christ. And it is also favoured when there is positive external change through good government. Both developments are now taking place in Colombia."

President Uribe bowed his head as I spoke a closing blessing that the Lord would watch over him, his family, his government and the nation of Colombia.

I retook my seat, conscious of how much God had watched over all of us too. I left the coliseum with hugs from my family and holding my grandsons. I "lifted my eyes" up to the beautiful hills around Bogotá. And I smiled.

Chapter 19
....

MORE BABIES AND A GLOBAL FAMILY

I T IS NOW OVER TEN YEARS since we lost Carol and a whole new life and lifestyle has emerged. Our close-knit family which was reduced from five to four has to date grown to fifteen, or seventeen including Gert and Lina.

Our children have been very obedient to the biblical command to "be fruitful and multiply". After the births of the "twin cousins", Samuel and Joseph, all three couples had more babies in 2009.

Samuel gained a brother when Wilana gave birth to Joshua William Erasmus early in the afternoon of 21 February. He weighed in at just under 8 lb (3.6 kg) and proceeded to grow at a rapid rate. At eighteen months he weighed the same as his brother who was two years older.

Joseph also gained a brother when Vasti gave birth to Joel Nathanael Braam (Afrikaans for Abraham) in the early hours of 26 April. Joel looked like James did as a baby and he soon followed his Dad's example as an infant by waking up several times a night, ready to play games. I tried not to smile too much as I told James how much I sympathized with his and his son's sleeplessness.

Melody and Drikus became parents for the first time at 8.31 a.m. on 17 July with the arrival of Isaac Johannes (Afrikaans for

John) Wesley Erasmus. From the first Mel proved to be a natural Mum. Drikus soon adapted, as he promised, "when the time came", to helping out with nappy changing, even though he usually pulled his shirt up to his face as a mask.

Nearly two years later, in 2011, all three couples were expecting again. When Wes and Wilana told me that they were going to have their third child I guessed, given previous form, that I would soon be getting similar calls from the other two couples. And so it proved. Without, I am assured, any prior arrangement between them, Mel and Vasti announced within a short space of each other that they were again pregnant. As the British columnist Littlejohn often writes: "You couldn't make it up."

Wes and Wilana led the way with the arrival of Daniel John Hendrikus on 5 April 2011. He was born eleven days prematurely at just over 6 lb 10 oz (3 kg). It wasn't long before he was happily trying to be part of the action with his energetic older brothers.

On 8 July 2011, exactly nine years to the day after Carol's funeral, my seventh grandson appeared. Caleb Johannes Andrew had kept Melody and Drikus waiting a while but he eventually weighed in at 8 lb 5 oz (3.8 kg). He was a good sleeper, which proved a blessing to me as well as his parents.

Over a month later, my first granddaughter arrived on 18 August – all 6 lb 11 oz (3.1 kg) of her, with a very full head of black hair, just like her mother Vasti, Carol's lookalike. James and Vasti named her a couple of days later as Eliana Maria Carol Richards. Eliana comes from a Hebrew word meaning "God has answered". All the family had moist eyes when we found we had another Carol Richards in the family.

I don't mind admitting that I have shed some tears at the arrival of each child. Usually I held it together until the parents put the latest newborn in my arms, and then I was done for.

I have often thought how much Carol would have revelled in all of this. She would have been in her element. We have all felt the pangs that she is not here to share it. But mostly we have celebrated all the new beginnings that have come to our family.

A decade on from what seemed to be a never-ending nightmare, so much has changed in our family and in our church family. Our home church has grown both in quality of community and in quantity of people, many of whom had no previous church background. I have never enjoyed being a pastor more. I'm so thankful for the privilege of ministering to such a genuine and committed group of people, so many of whom stood by us in our darkest moments.

In South Africa, we formally joined together with our African church family. King's Church International, Robertson was launched on Sunday, 29 March 2009 with an announcement that this was not an Afrikaner church nor an English church but a church where "all races are welcome and our vision is for the whole world".

Since then we have seen a lot of growth, particularly in our distinctive second service for children which has just over a thousand regular attendees, mostly from the poorer, rural areas, who we bus into town. We also feed them each week and have an ongoing clothing programme. For our big Easter and Christmas services we hire the local rugby stadium.

A similar number of children regularly attend a kids' service which our children's pastor, Paul Bristow, pioneered in Burkina Faso, one of the world's poorest nations, where we have been involved for many years in supporting educational, health and church development projects.

We feel like we have also been "adopted" into a wider international family, as our friendships in Colombia have led to many others in Latin America, North America, Asia, Africa, Europe and in the UK.

Pastor César Castellanos was with us, along with many international friends, for a special service on Sunday, 1 November 2009 at Windsor's Parish Church, where we had attended Carol's funeral. On this occasion Pastor César said he was going to do something that he had never done before in all his years of global ministry. He was going to "anoint" an entire family as pastors.

And so, in a memorable commissioning service, Wes and Wilana, James and Vasti, Drikus and Mel, along with Gert and Lina, Terry and Margaret (our faithful friends and church leaders) and myself, knelt down on the same stage where Carol's coffin had rested while Pastor César prayed over us and anointed us with oil.

What had happened in our family, Pastor César said, was a sign that God wanted to heal many families, in a nation of broken families.

Chapter 20

EPILOGUE

OVER THE PAST DECADE so much has taken place that I could not have even attempted to make up or imagine.

I never imagined that I would have to face the deep loss of my closest friend and the love of my life so early in life.

I never imagined how I would get over such an emotionally demoralizing blow.

I never imagined how a family who had gone through such sadness could come to experience such happiness.

I never imagined how so much good could come out of so much bad.

I never dreamt that one day I would have a lot of little guys running around calling me Grandad or that my reasonably ordered home could be so quickly reduced to such chaos and fun when they all pitch up – which they do frequently, as all the kids live within a few miles of me.

I never imagined that out of our vulnerability we would stand together as a family and that all the couples would serve together as pastors in church ministry both at home and abroad.

I never imagined that when I felt like shutting up shop and staying at home, I would travel to more nations than ever before to bring a message of hope and healing.

I never imagined that I would become a father figure to

many wonderful spiritual sons and daughters from near and far who were "born in the time of our bereavement".[18]

And I never imagined just how true the Bible is when it says that God is able to do immeasurably more than all that we can ask or imagine.

Of course, there have been sad and lonely moments over this past ten years. I still miss Carol deeply. But I no longer grieve as I did for what is lost.

There is, for sure, no future in living in the past. I want to make the most of each day. I look forward with hope.

And I want you to do so as well. That's the main reason why I wanted to write this book.

I don't know what your circumstances are. What you have gone through or are going through may be far more painful than anything I have gone through.

I know all too well that there are no quick fixes.

I know that some things in life will never be the same when you have been hit by traumatic winds of change.

But I want you to know that your life can turn around.

I want you to know that there can come peace in your storm and calm after your storm.

I want you to know that you can recover from your pain.

I want you to know that joy can be restored to you.

Just because you are down, it doesn't mean that you are out. You may think that your life is finished. But the reality may very well be that a life you never imagined is only just beginning.

You may have had a big setback, but you can make a big comeback.

You too may have had tough times, but better times are ahead.

You may be vulnerable, but great strength can grow out of

---

18   Isaiah 49:20.

your extreme weakness.

Your great trouble can shape you up for great blessing.

For sure, there is a time to live and a time to die, but you need to make sure that you don't give up and die when you still have so much to live for.

You may not think you have any bright prospects right now, but you will never discover what goodness and mercy is ahead of you if you stop moving forward.

You may be much nearer to making it through than you know.

You need to hang in there when it's dark and hold on when everything is telling you to let go.

I say that because I believe there is great resilience in the human spirit. So often it is only in times of crisis that you discover strengths that you and others never imagined that you possessed.

More than ever, I believe that there is great power when we exercise our wills and make a conscious decision to persevere and focus on what we have and not on what we have lost.

And I believe that there is great creative power for good when we determine to speak positively in negative circumstances. As Proverbs 18:21 puts it, "The tongue has the power of life and death."

But above all, I also say that you must not quit because I believe that there is a God and that He answers and rewards those who seek Him and trust Him.

So often you can't plan for what may happen in your life, but I believe that God nevertheless has a plan for your life.

I am all too well aware that there is so much we don't know and can't explain about suffering. I am old enough, have read enough, seen enough and lived through enough not to pretend to have any smart answers.

But some things I do know. "I know," as Job said in the long night of his suffering, "that my Redeemer lives" (Job 19:25).

I know that God is for me, even when circumstances have been against me.

I know, and our family knows through shared experiences, that what the psalmist said long ago is for real. God "is close to the brokenhearted and saves those who are crushed in spirit" (Psalm 34:18).

If I didn't know that, I wouldn't have written this book.

I believe that God is a good God who wants to help us through our greatest trials. He is not the author of evil and He has the power to deliver us from evil.

I believe that "God is a very present help in time of trouble" and that "therefore we should not fear" (Psalm 46:1–2).

I believe that there is no circumstance that need separate us from the love of God. Or, as the late great old lady, Corrie ten Boom, survivor of the horrors of Ravensbrück concentration camp, used to say: "There is no pit so deep that His love is not deeper still."[19]

I believe that Jesus Christ is the ultimate example of that love.

I believe that in His life he had compassion for all kinds of people and that He reached out to the hurting, harassed and hungry to meet their needs.

I believe that through His death on the cross He not only paid the price of our sin but He has also "borne our griefs and carried our sorrows" (Isaiah 53:4, NKJV).

I believe that because of His actual, physical resurrection from the dead, He has the power bring us all into a new day of comfort and confidence, both for this life and the life to come.

---

19 Corrie ten Boom, widely quoted, including in *The Hiding Place*, London: Hodder & Stoughton.

And I believe that even when we lose loved ones or when people forsake us, Jesus is the greatest friend we could ever have. I am still moved by the words of an old hymn:

> *What a friend we have in Jesus*
> *All our sins and griefs to bear*
> *What a privilege to carry*
> *Everything to God in prayer.*[20]

Somehow, when we draw near to God in simple prayer, He draws near to us. It's when we lay down our unanswerable questions and decide to trust God with a childlike, rather than a childish, faith that we begin to discover just what a never-failing friend He is.

What I have experienced over many years and what you too can discover is summed up in the words of one of my favourite worship songs, by Reuben Morgan:

> *You are my strength*
> *Strength like no other*
> *Strength like no other*
> *Reaches to me*
>
> *You are my hope*
> *Hope like no other*
> *Hope like no other*
> *Reaches to me*
>
> *In the fullness of Your grace*
> *In the power of Your name*
> *You lift me up*
> *You lift me up*

---

20 Joseph Medlicott Scriven (1819–1886), "What a friend we have in Jesus".

Unfailing love
Stronger than mountains
Deeper than oceans
Reaches to me

Your love O Lord
Reaches to the heavens
Your faithfulness
Reaches to the skies[21]

I pray that will be your experience also. Your heart can be healed. You can know the unconditional and never-failing love of the Good Shepherd who comes looking for us and carries us to safety in this life and the next.

You can know the saving and sustaining grace of God Almighty.

You are not alone. You are not finished. You are going to make it. You have hope and a future.

21 Reuben Morgan, "You are my strength", Copyright © 2007 Hillsong Music Publishing.

FREE AT LAST

By Carol Richards

An excerpt from Carol's last talk at a women's conference that she led. The conference theme was: "Free at Last".

I FEEL THE LORD HAS TOLD ME just to scrap my introduction and to share something that I hadn't intended to share, so I hope I can say it.

As you know, if you are planning something like this, you have to plan months ahead. Well, my Dad died in January and that was about the time when I thought I would begin to plan this conference. And I think the reason that I am telling you that is because things like this happen to us in life.

Sickness happens to us. Circumstances come that are out of our control. But I think that what matters in those times is how we react in those circumstances.

If we close down in those times, if we shut off from what God wants to do with us, then we become hard and the Lord's not able to walk through that with us. And I feel that He wants to tell us to be open to Him in those difficult times, so that He can walk with us and bring us into His freedom and into His purposes.

HOPE AND A FUTURE FOR YOU

> *"For I know the plans I have for you," declares the*
> *LORD, "plans to prosper you and not to harm you,*
> *plans to give you hope and a future. Then you will call*
> *on me and come and pray to me, and I will listen to*
> *you. You will seek me and find me when you seek me*
> *with all your heart."*

These inspiring verses from Jeremiah 29:11–13 show that our experience of discovering hope and a future is linked to our heartfelt desire to know God and our response to God.

The Bible makes clear that God has no favourites and that anyone who sincerely and humbly seeks Him can find Him.

In the Sermon on the Mount Jesus said: "Ask and it will be given to you; seek and you will find; knock and the door will be opened to you. For everyone who asks receives; the one who seeks finds; and to the one who knocks, the door will be opened" Matthew 7:7–8.

I believe that God is "only a prayer away". I encourage you to speak out this prayer:

> *Lord Jesus, I need your help. I choose to believe that*
> *you died on the Cross and rose again from the dead so*
> *that I can have a new beginning.*
>
> *So please forgive me for my sins and heal my*
> *heart. Change me from the inside out.*

*From today on I am going to rely on you and
truly follow you. Please come close to me. Give me
daily strength so that I know I have hope and a future.
Amen.*

If you pray and mean a prayer like that, God will hear and answer your prayer. It will be the start of a new life and new lifestyle. Jesus compared it to being "born again".

We have had enough babies in our family to know that exciting as it is to have these new arrivals, they also need a lot of care and nurturing.

That's why you will need to find a church "family" who will love you unconditionally. A good church will help you to develop in your Christian commitment and in an ever increasing experience of the goodness and grace of God. Do your best to find a life-giving church in your area.

If you want any further information on how to grow as a Christian, we'd love to hear from you and give you any help we can.

Please contact us at www.kcionline.org or at www.hopeandafuture.info

KING'S CHURCH INTERNATIONAL

About King's Church International

King's Church International (KCI) is a non-denominational local church with a global vision.

UK

King's Church International is based in Windsor, home of Her Majesty the Queen and close to London.

Sunday services are held at Holy Trinity Garrison Church in Windsor.

Members of King's Church International also meet in over 100 small groups that are aimed at the promotion of positive change in individuals, families, communities and cultures.

Africa

In South Africa, King's Church International is based in Robertson, near Cape Town. As in the UK, the church is multi-racial with a strong involvement in the local community, particularly among children, youth and families. Over 1000 children attend Sunday services.

For nearly two decades King's Church International has been a major supporter of 600 children and six schools in Burkina Faso, one of the world's poorest countries.

Other links

King's Church International works closely with partner churches in Colombo, Sri Lanka and St Louis, USA.

KCI also has strong links to one of the fastest growing churches in the world, MCI in Bogotá, Colombia and its network of churches around the world.

King's Church International is a member of the Evangelical Alliance, which represents over 1.2 million Christians in the UK.

For many years KCI has worked with Alpha International, founded by Holy Trinity Brompton, London, in promoting the Alpha course, an introduction to Christianity.

For more information and details of weekly podcasts, please visit:
Web: www.kcionline.org
Facebook: www.facebook.com/kingschurchinternational
Twitter: @kingschurch